International Compliance 101

How to build and maintain an effective compliance and ethics program

By
Debbie Troklus
and
Sheryl Vacca

Copyright © 2013 by the Society of Corporate Compliance & Ethics

Printed in the United States of America. All rights reserved. This book or parts thereof may not be reproduced in any form without the express written permission of the publisher.

ISBN 978-0-9792210-7-1

This publication is designed to provide accurate and authoritative information in regard to the subject matter covered. It is sold with the understanding that neither the author nor the publisher is engaged in rendering legal, accounting, or other professional service. If legal advice or other expert assistance is required, the services of a competent professional person should be sought (from a Declaration of Principles jointly adopted by a Committee of the American Bar Association and a Committee of Publishers).

To order copies of this publication, please contact:

Society of Corporate Compliance & Ethics
6500 Barrie Road, Suite 250
Minneapolis, MN 55435
Phone: +1 952 933 4977
Fax: +1 952 988 0146
Web site: www.corporatecompliance.org
e-mail: info@corporatecompliance.org

Contents

INTRODUCTION: What's in a Name? v

CHAPTER 1: What Is a Compliance Program? 1
   Who Needs a Compliance Program 1
   Why Compliance Programs are Essential 3
   Top Reasons to Implement a Compliance Program 3
   Still More Compliance Program Benefits 6

CHAPTER 2: The Seven Essential Elements 7
   1. Standards of Conduct/Policies and Procedures 7
   2. Compliance Officer and Compliance Committee 12
   3. Education 17
   4. Monitoring and Auditing 21
   5. Reporting and Investigating 27
   6. Enforcement and Discipline 31
   7. Response and Prevention 34

CHAPTER 3: Organizational Steps 39
   1. Gain Support and Commitment 39
   2. Establish Financial Support 42
   3. Develop a Code of Conduct 47
   4. Identify Staffing Needs 50
   5. Conduct Internal Risk Assessment 51
   6. Develop Mission and Goals 54
   7. Next Steps After Implementation 56

CHAPTER 4: Tailoring Your Compliance Program 59
    1. Communication 59
    2. Continual Evaluation 60
    3. Measuring Effectiveness 61
    4. Organizational Fit 63
    5. Advancing Your Program 64
    6. Change 64
    7. Compliance Program Breaking Points 65

Epilogue **69**

Appendices **71**
    A.1: Sample Letter to Vendors 72
    A.2: Sample Non-Retaliation/Non-Retribution Policy 73
    A.3: Sample Search Warrant Response Policy
        (might not apply in some countries) 76
    A.4: Sample Compliance Officer Job Description 80
    A.5: Sample Audit Review Form 85
    A.6: Sample Confidentiality Statement 86
    A.7: Sample Complaint Information Sheet 87
    A.8: Sample Compliance Issue Follow-Up Form 88
    A.9: Audit Review Plan Templates 89
    A.10: Sample Board of Directors Resolution 92
    B: Code of Ethics for Compliance and Ethics Professionals 96

Glossary of Compliance Terms **105**

Endnotes **110**

About the Authors **111**

Introduction

What's in A Name?

You may have noticed that some organizations have compliance programs, others have integrity or ethics programs. They are often considered synonymous, but a subtle distinction can be made between the two terms. It is generally thought that the title "compliance program" implies a primary concern with following rules and regulations, whereas the title "integrity or ethics program" puts the emphasis on values and doing the right thing. There may be differences in approach and subtleties of content, but there are basic elements common to both compliance and integrity/ethics programs. Those common elements, whatever the title of the program, are the focus of this book, although for convenience's sake the term "compliance program" will be used throughout. Each organization must pick a title—or perhaps create an entirely new title—depending on its needs and culture.

You may not be aware of it, but there are probably many compliance activities already occurring in your organization. Across the world, regulations such as anti-corruption, wage and hour rules, and environmental health and safety are all compliance-related activities. Moreover, each and every industry is subject to the regulations and guidance of regulatory bodies specific to their industry and countries of operation. Finally, all organizations must maintain compliance with contract law and the agreements that they make with suppliers, competitors, customers, and other stakeholders. Through the implementation of a formal compliance program you will be able to demonstrate to regulatory bodies and stakeholders that your organization is committed to act in accordance with the rules set out for the industry, geographic location and the arrangements to which all have agreed. Should any of your organization's employees not be acting appropriately, this will more readily be discovered and resolved through the compliance program as well.

The focus of this book is on compliance for organizations that conduct business internationally. It is recognized that the type of organization may be U.S.-based, and/or country-specific with operations in several different countries globally.

1

What Is a Compliance Program?

There are many definitions of a compliance program. On a very basic level it is about education, definition, prevention, detection, collaboration, and enforcement. It is a system of individuals, processes, and policies and procedures developed to ensure compliance with all applicable laws, industry regulations, and private contracts governing the actions of the organization. A compliance program is not merely a binder on a shelf and it is not a quick fix to the latest risk areas. A compliance program—an *effective* compliance program—must be engrained in the culture and an ongoing process that is part of the fabric of the organization. A compliance program must be a commitment to an ethical way of conducting business and a system for helping individuals to do the right thing.

Who Needs a Compliance Program
- Private Businesses
- Publicly Traded Companies
- Foundations and other Non-Profit Organizations
- Government Agencies
- Schools
- Others.

So, why do we need yet another formal program—this time on compliance?

First and foremost, an effective compliance program safeguards the organization's legal responsibility to abide by applicable laws and regulations. Any organization that has international operations must stay current with applicable laws and regulations in each country in which it does business. Recent trends in regulations include:

- Increased anti-corruption enforcement—e.g., the Foreign Corruption Protection Act (FCPA) in the US, the UK Bribery Act in the UK, and the strengthened anti-corruption standards established by the Organisation for Economic Cooperation and Development (OECD)

- Global growth of antitrust laws and regulations—more than 100 countries now have penalties for anti-competition behavior

- Increased protection of whistleblowers—e.g., the Dodd-Frank Wall Street Reform Act in the US

- Increased privacy and data protection regulations—e.g., the European Union's 1995 Data Protection Directive and Charter of Fundamental Rights of the EU, the Asia-Pacific Economic Cooperation's (APEC's) Privacy Framework, the Payment Card Industry (PCI) Data Security Standard in the US, etc.

Other benefits for having a compliance program include the ability to:

- Demonstrate to employees and the community the organization's commitment to good corporate conduct

- Identify and prevent criminal and unethical conduct

- Create a centralized source of information on industry regulations

- Develop a methodology that encourages employees to report potential problems

- Develop procedures that allow the prompt, thorough investigation of alleged misconduct

- Initiate immediate and appropriate corrective action
- Reduce the organization's exposure to enforcement sanctions.

While a compliance program may require significant additional resources or reallocation of existing resources to implement an effective compliance program, the long-term benefits of implementing the program outweigh the costs. An effective compliance program is a sound investment.

Why Compliance Programs are Essential

- To protect reputation or the organization
- To encourage a culture of "doing the right thing"
- To increase awareness both for employees and stakeholders
- To provide an avenue for employees and stakeholders to raise potential issues
- To reduce the imposition of fines and sentences.

Top Reasons to Implement a Compliance Program

1. Adopting a compliance program concretely demonstrates to the community at large that an organization has a strong commitment to honesty and responsible corporate citizenship. One of the company's greatest assets is its reputation and, once damaged, one of the most difficult to repair. An effective compliance program can both preserve and enhance an entity's reputation by preventing fraud and abuse and/or by discovering inappropriate actions early and resolving them in a timely and proper manner.

2. Compliance programs reinforce employees' innate sense of right and wrong. People have an inherent sense of right and wrong and want a means to respond to conduct they perceive to be noncompliant. By providing employees with ways to express concerns to management and to see a positive response, providers strengthen the relationship of trust with their employees. This can be done with compliance tools such as codes of conduct and training.

3. **Compliance programs are cost-effective.** Although an effective compliance program requires a commitment of significant resources, those expenditures are insignificant in comparison to the disruption and expense of defending against a fraud investigation. Moreover, the increased communication and monitoring of operations and financials, which results from compliance activities, can create efficiencies and more streamlined processes.

4. **A compliance program provides a more accurate view of employee and third party agent behavior relating to fraud and abuse.** An effective compliance program provides ongoing training of employees and suppliers, monitors their understanding and compliance with the program, and provides the mechanisms to discipline those individuals who violate the company's code of conduct. It is through these vehicles that an organization can have reasonable assurances that it is acting in conformance with applicable rules.

5. **A compliance program provides procedures to promptly correct misconduct.** A comprehensive compliance program provides established procedures for promptly and efficiently responding to problems that may arise. Through early detection and reporting, a company can minimize the penalties and sanctions imposed by regulatory bodies, and/or the fines and repercussions of violating contracts. Thereby, companies can reduce their exposure to penalties, and criminal and administrative sanctions.

6. **Voluntarily implementing a compliance program is preferable to waiting for a mandate by a regulatory body.** Voluntary programs are preferable due to their flexibility to adapt to the organization's culture. In designing a voluntary program you have the ability to decide what the structure will be. When you design the program, you also have the ability to gain a greater level of buy-in from all levels of the employees throughout the organization. Voluntary compliance programs demonstrate to your stakeholders your commitment to "doing the right thing" because you want to be a "good faith organization" and not doing this because you "have to."

7. **Effective corporate compliance programs may protect corporate directors (board members, shareholders) from personal liability.** The fiduciary duties of corporate directors require that they keep themselves adequately informed concerning the operations and finances of the company. An effective compliance program designed to assure compliance with applicable legal requirements has been recognized as meeting this duty of care.

Avoidance of penalties and fines should be a major incentive for organizations to implement a compliance program. Should an organization be found guilty of fraud, the penalties can be severe. The financial implications due to loss of business can be profound.

Although a "one size fits all" compliance program does not exist, many industries have accepted seven basic compliance elements that can be tailored to fit the needs and financial realities of any given organization. Effective compliance programs begin with a formal commitment to these basic elements. The seven basic compliance program elements are:

1. Written standards of conduct and policies and procedures
2. Designation of a chief compliance officer and other appropriate bodies
3. Effective education and training
4. Audits and evaluation techniques to monitor compliance
5. Establishment of reporting processes and procedures for complaints
6. Appropriate disciplinary mechanisms
7. Investigation and remediation of systemic problems.

Once a program has been established, the program information and relevant regulatory materials should be distributed, read, and studied carefully by all employees of an organization, as they make up the backbone of a good compliance program.

Still More Compliance Program Benefits

- Preventing false or inaccurate financial statements from being generated and published

- Fulfilling the fundamental mission of the organization through ethical business conduct and business efficiency

- Demonstrating to employees and the community the organization's strong commitment to honest and responsible conduct

- Providing a more accurate view of employee and supplier behavior related to fraud and abuse

- Improving overall communication between and within departments

- Identifying and preventing inappropriate and unethical conduct

- Improving financial performance

- Encouraging employees to report potential fraud

- Allowing for thorough investigations of suspected inappropriate actions

- Providing an "early warning" system for identifying problems

- Minimizing an organization's exposure to various criminal damages and penalties

- Minimizing an organization's exposure to *qui tam* or whistleblower suits or other actions of frustrated or disgruntled employees.

2

The Seven Essential Elements

1. Standards of Conduct/Policies and Procedures

The first of the basic compliance elements in industry guidance recommends that the organization establish standards and procedures to prevent and detect criminal conduct. The standards or code of conduct and the policies and procedures become the tools with which you can build your compliance program.

The standards of conduct, first and foremost, demonstrate the organization's overarching ethical attitude and its organization-wide emphasis on compliance with all applicable laws and regulations. The code is meant for all employees and all representatives of the organization. This includes management, vendors, suppliers, and those who are working on behalf of an organization, which are frequently overlooked groups. From the board of directors to volunteers, everyone must receive, read, understand, and agree to abide by the standards of the code of conduct. For this reason the code should be written plainly and concisely in an accessible style. An easy-to-understand reading level is recommended. Plain and concise does not mean generic, however. The contents of the code of conduct will need to be tailored to the organization's culture, business, and corporate identity. Also, institutions with a diverse constituency should consider providing the code of conduct in other languages, sign language, or even Braille as appropriate. When providing the code in different translations, the organization should "test" that the translation is accurate.

Establishing an organization-wide code of conduct is a key recommendation of the Organisation for Economic Cooperation and Development (OECD), which in 2010, established the "Good Practice Guidance on Internal Controls, Ethics and Compliance." The OECD's Working Group on Bribery, which authored the Guidance, urges companies to establish:

1. Strong, explicit and visible support and commitment from senior management to the company's internal controls, ethics and compliance programmes or measures for preventing and detecting foreign bribery;

2. A clearly articulated and visible corporate policy prohibiting foreign bribery....[1]

The OECD's Guidance is contained in its 2009 Anti-Bribery Convention, an internationally recognized document that has been ratified by its 34 member countries and six non-member countries[2]. While its primary focus is on preventing bribery, the Convention supports compliance programs with a larger focus, stating that its recommendations "should be interconnected with a company's overall compliance framework."[3]

The code of conduct provides a process for proper decision-making, for doing the right thing. It elevates corporate performance in basic business relationships and confirms that the organization upholds and supports proper compliance conduct. Managers should be encouraged to refer to the code of conduct whenever possible, incorporating elements or standards into performance reviews. Compliance with the standards must be enforced through appropriate discipline when necessary. Disciplinary procedures should be clearly stated in the standards, and the penalty—up to and including dismissal—for serious violations of the standards of conduct must be mentioned to emphasize the organization's commitment. *(See Element Number 6 – Enforcement and Discipline.)*

Code of Conduct—Content Checklist

- Demonstrates an organizational emphasis on compliance with all applicable laws and regulations
- Is written plainly and concisely so all employees can understand the standards

- Is translated into other languages, as appropriate
- Includes frequently asked questions or scenarios based on high risk areas
- Includes expectations for employees on interactions with other employees, suppliers and clients
- Mentions organizational policies without completely restating them
- Is consistent with company policies and procedures
- Includes management's responsibility to explain and enforce the code.

Code of Conduct—Communicating to Employees

- All employees must receive and read the standards
- A supervisor or qualified trainer should explain the standards and answer any questions
- Employees should attest in writing that they have received, read, and understood the standards
- Employee compliance with the standards must be enforced through appropriate discipline when necessary
- Noncompliance with the standards will be disciplined and this should be clearly stated.

Code of Conduct—Purpose

- To present overarching guidelines for employees to follow
- To clearly state expectations for all employees to understand what is required of them
- To provide a process for proper decision-making
- To assure that employees put standards into everyday practice
- To elevate the organization's performance in basic business relationships
- To confirm that the organization upholds and supports proper compliance conduct.

(See Appendix A.1, Sample Letter to Vendors.)

Policies and Procedures

Whereas a code of conduct provides guidelines for business decision-making and behavior, the compliance policies and procedures are specific and address identified areas of risk. Most organizations already have an employee manual that outlines all human resource-related policies and procedures, and they may have other operational policies and procedures specific to certain business practices or operations. Whenever possible, compliance policies and procedures should be integrated into existing policies, and all policies within an organization should be consistent with laws, regulations, industry requirements, and general compliance. In fact, as part of the implementation of a compliance program and while in the process of drafting compliance policies and procedures, all other policies within the organization should be reviewed and revised as necessary. While it is imperative that the organization have policies and procedures, it cannot be emphasized enough that the only thing worse than not having a policy is having a policy and not following it.

Develop your policies and procedures carefully. Take care that they are realistic and measurable. Be sure your goals are realistic.

Two types of compliance policies and procedures should be developed by every organization: structural and substantive. The structural policies create the basic framework of how the compliance program will operate. The substantive policies define the applicable regulations that apply to the organization and how to operate compliantly within those regulations. They also indicate the applicable risk areas to an organization and describe appropriate and inappropriate behaviors with regard to those risk areas. Both the structural and the substantive policies and procedures are essential to a compliance program so that the rules to which employees will be held and the method for enforcing the rules are clearly documented.

Structural policies and procedures should be developed to address:

- Directives or mission of the compliance program

- Revision of existing and creation of new policies and procedures (including distribution and updating requirements)

- Role of the compliance officer

- Role of the compliance committee

- Educational requirements.

- Method for anonymous reporting and non-retaliation for reporting: It is important to have a clearly stated policy on non-retaliation and non-retribution in the organization. Let everyone know there will be no retaliation or retribution for bringing forth problems.

- Auditing processes

- Monitoring processes

- Method for responding to reports of possible misconduct

- Method for responding to internal and external requests for documents or other investigations

- Disciplinary action plan which is consistent with HR processes and/or policy

- Anonymous reporting mechanism, if applicable to your organization and country in which the business is located

- Record retention/destruction.

Substantive policies and procedures should be developed to address:

- Process for preventing inappropriate actions in specific risk areas for which there are not already policies to address those areas; e.g., conflict of interest, privacy and security of information, intellectual property, export controls, etc.

- Key risk areas where an organization may not have a defined policy and/or business owner; e.g., conflicts of interest, privacy and security of information, etc.

- Documentation requirements.

Policies and procedures, like the code of conduct, must be living documents, not just a binder on a shelf. They must become integral to the day-to-day operation of the organization. That is what forms the basis for an effective compliance program. To determine if that goal is met, consider: How are the policies and procedures applied every day? Are they incorporated into performance reviews? Educational programs? Are they reviewed and updated according to a schedule and on time? Revising policies and procedures is a complex and ongoing process and requires periodic review and revisions to assure they are current. Again, standards of conduct, policies, and procedures are the tools of compliance, but they must be used and sharpened to be effective.

2. Compliance Officer and Compliance Committee

Industry standards recommend designation of a compliance officer to serve as the focal point for compliance activities. Whether the position is full time or part time will depend on the size, scope, and resources of the organization. In most cases, the position should be a full time role and an organization will determine the feasibility and scalability of dedicating resources. Also, assigning the compliance officer appropriate authority is critical to the success of the program. On a specific level, for example, the compliance officer must have full authority to access any and all documents that are relevant to compliance activities. This includes documents such as financial statements and supporting documents, contracts with suppliers and agents, and other accounting records. In the big picture, however, "appropriate authority" comes from the unquestionable backing by the CEO and board of directors or its equivalent, the sources of ultimate authority and respect.

Appropriate authority and the full backing of the board of directors and management are consistent with industry practice. To carry out such operational responsibility, such individual(s) should be given adequate resources, appropriate authority, and direct access to the governing authority or an appropriate subgroup of the governing authority. This is logical because it is the board that supported the launch of the compliance initiative and approved the hiring of the compliance officer. Board members may even be actively involved in the interviewing of the compliance officer candidates. They also should be involved in the development of the compliance officer's job description, and an important part of the compliance officer's reporting structure.

There is concern and some risk involved in having the compliance officer report to general counsel or to the chief financial officer. This reporting arrangement creates real and/or potential appearance of conflict of interest due to their respective roles with management. Separation of compliance from legal and finance when possible, helps ensure that all aspects of the compliance officer's role will be independent and objective (meaning there is no real or perceived vested interest in the outcome). There are different reporting structures for the compliance officer role and many variables have to be considered by the organization for determining what works best for the individual organization. However, the dominant theme in industry on the reporting structure is for the compliance officer to report directly to the organization CEO and/or the internal governing body (e.g., oversight committee, supervisory board, administrative body, board of directors, audit committee) to maintain their real and/or perceived independence. The size and setting of your organization will influence its reporting structure. It is recommended that the board or its liaison committee have, at minimum, a "dotted line" or indirect reporting relationship with the compliance officer. See below a snapshot view of compliance officer reporting structures, from a 2010 survey conducted by the Society of Corporate Compliance and Ethics and the Health Care Compliance Association.

Compliance Officer Reporting Structures[4]

	Type of Organization in Which Respondent Works				
				Total	
To Whom Compliance Officer Reports	For profit, publicly traded	For profit, privately held	Non-profit	Number	%
Board	31	51	183	256	55.6%
Chief Executive Officer	14	23	79	116	24.4%
Chief Financial Officer	3	5	11	19	4.0%
General Counsel	16	8	14	38	8.0%
Human Resources	0	0	0	0	0%
Other	11	6	22	39	8.1%

The compliance officer's duties also will vary depending on size and scope of the program. The main focus of the position should be the implementation, administration, and oversight of the compliance program. Primary responsibilities should include the following:

- Designing, implementing, overseeing, and monitoring the compliance program

- Reporting on a regular basis to the organization's governing body, CEO, and compliance committee

- Revising the compliance program periodically as appropriate

- Developing, coordinating, and participating in a multifaceted educational and training program

- Ensuring that those we do business with are aware of the organization's compliance program requirements

- Serving as a source of compliance-related information for employees, management, suppliers, and the board

- Ensuring that appropriate background checks are conducted according to country specific regulations

- Assisting with internal compliance review and monitoring activities

- Assuring management has mechanisms in place to mitigate risks

- Independently investigating and acting on matters related to compliance

- Assuring management takes corrective action to resolve the problems identified

- Assuring the organization has given employees a mechanism for reporting potential issues.

The compliance officer is a unique position requiring an individual who understands the nature of the business or industry, is capable of understanding and questioning practices in the organization, including financial areas, is knowledgeable of applicable legal requirements that may be imposed in the industry for wrongdoing, has strong written and verbal communication skills, and is firm yet approachable. Whatever the tenure or the educational level, the compliance officer, as "focal point" of the program, must be a figure respected and trusted throughout the organization. Strong interpersonal skills, good listening abilities, and discretion are mandatory. (*See Appendix A.4, Sample Compliance Officer Job Description.*)

As compliance has grown and matured as a profession, it has, like other professions, sought to identify and distinguish those in the field who have, with experience and education, achieved the necessary skill set to be an effective compliance officer.

Moreover, compliance officers are also stewards of a public trust, and therefore the services provided must be of the highest standards of professionalism, integrity, and competence. The Code of Ethics for Compliance Professionals *(see Appendix B)* addresses three principles, which are broad standards of an inspirational nature. They include:

Principle I: Obligations to the Public—Compliance and ethics professionals (CEPs) should abide by and promote compliance with the spirit and the letter of the law governing their employing organization's conduct and exemplify the highest ethical standards in their professional conduct in order to contribute to the public good.

Principle II: Obligations to the Employing Organization—Compliance and ethics professionals (CEPs) should serve their employing organizations with the highest sense of integrity, exercise unprejudiced and unbiased judgment on their behalf, and promote effective compliance and ethics programs.

Principle III: Obligation to the Profession—Compliance and ethics professionals (CEPs) should strive, through their actions, to uphold the integrity and dignity of the profession, to advance the effectiveness of compliance and ethics programs, and to promote professionalism in compliance and ethics.

These principles and the accompanying rules of conduct should be reviewed and studied—and adhered to—by all compliance officers.

The compliance officer may be the focal point of a compliance program, but he or she cannot be the only point, nor does this role "assure" compliance for the organization. Industry has demonstrated that the formation of a compliance committee can be an effective addition to the program, although the specific composition of the committee may vary. The committee will benefit from having varying perspectives such as operations, finance, audit, human resources, and legal, as well as employees and managers of key operating units. This committee will assist the compliance officer in ensuring effective mechanisms are in place to mitigate risk areas, real and/or potential.

The compliance officer's role with the compliance committee can also vary. In some organizations the compliance officer sits *ex officio*. In others, the compliance officer may even chair the committee. Regardless of who chairs the committee, the compliance department commonly is responsible for scheduling meetings, preparing the agenda, taking and distributing minutes, and coordinating follow-up.

Compliance committee functions, in addition to aiding and supporting the compliance officer, can include the following:

- Analyzing legal requirements and specific risk areas

- Regularly reviewing and assessing the accuracy of and adherence to policies and procedures

- Assisting with the development of standards of conduct and policies and procedures

- Monitoring internal systems related to standards, policies, and procedures

- Reviewing industry guidance and new information regularly and integrating it into the compliance program

- Determining the appropriate strategy to promote compliance

- Developing a system to solicit, evaluate, and respond to complaints and problems.

The importance and potential influence of the compliance committee cannot be overstated. Look for committed individuals who will be strong, visible, and vocal advocates for the compliance program. Furthermore, the committee should be composed of individuals representative of each unique department in the organization so that they can communicate to the rest of the committee and the compliance officer the compliance activities and risk areas within their department. The members are also important in providing communication back to their respective departments on the organization's compliance requirements. The committee is a vital source of information both to the compliance officer and the rest of the organization.

3. Education

Education and training are the first and possibly the most important lines of defense for a compliance program. In a time where there are strong enforcement initiatives governing industry and business practices, education is the best strategy for prevention. It is suggested that the training be separated into two types, the first a general session on compliance for all employees and the second covering more specific information for appropriate personnel.

Ten Things to Include in Your Basic Compliance Course (these are suggestions which could be included but not limited to):

1. The body of legal and regulatory knowledge guiding all compliance activity
2. Your organization's specific compliance philosophy
3. How to handle compliance communication within and outside of your organization
4. How compliance violations are defined and how they should be reported
5. Policies regarding confidentiality

6. Policies regarding data privacy and security
7. Third-party relationships and relevant regulatory guidances
8. Steps for discipline of employees involved in compliance violations
9. Proper preparation of required filings
10. Proper retention of documents.

General training sessions are meant to heighten awareness among all employees and communicate and emphasize (and then update and reiterate) the organization's commitment to ethical business behavior, which affects all employees. An organization may be required to conduct training due to a contractual requirement or third-party mandate, but regardless, employees should be required to have a specific number of educational hours per year, as appropriate. For a frame of reference, a minimum of one hour annually for basic training in compliance areas should be required for any compliance program. As noted earlier, all employees should receive a copy of the standards of conduct and the key compliance policies and procedures. These, plus basic information about the organization's compliance program and how it operates, and how issues can be brought forward, are the core of general training.

Specific training in high-risk areas is critical for specialized personnel. These employees should be given specific training regarding how to properly perform their job functions as well as general compliance training with an emphasis on compliance risk areas specific to these employees' job functions. This specific training, above and beyond the general compliance training, may be more appropriate to provide in the form of one-on-one or on-the-job training to ensure that compliance is integrated into the employee's daily activities and doesn't remain a theoretical concept. It is not as effective to discuss and learn complex compliance risk areas through a computer-based program. The internal governing board should be trained on their role in oversight of the compliance program and compliance-related risks. Clarifying and emphasizing these areas of concern through training and educational programs are particularly relevant to specific roles in the organization; i.e., marketing, finance, sales, etc. The pressure to meet business goals may render these employees vulnerable to engaging in prohibited practices.

A written annual education plan should outline individual department content needs, timing, methods, and duration of training, and a strategy for securing managerial buy-in. Managers will need specific training on their role in the compliance program and the value of their support and participation. "Tone in the middle" cannot be overlooked.

An uncooperative manager can, directly or indirectly, consciously or unconsciously, deter staff from attending. The manager must emphasize the importance of training by encouraging and facilitating employee attendance. Adult learning styles vary. Some learn through listening, others through seeing, and many by doing. So, to keep education vital and engaging to a diversified staff, the key is to develop a variety of educational formats—videos, lectures, brown bag lunches, roundtable discussions. "Lunch and Learn" sessions and roundtable discussion can be especially effective in targeting a specific training need, and they can provide education regarding the reality of what is going on in the departments to the trainers and ultimately to compliance personnel. Your organization may already have various forums you can tap into, such as department meetings or all-staff meetings for targeted education. Use of web training applications that can provide practice solving "virtual" scenarios has also become popular. Look for ways compliance education can fit into the ways staff are being educated on other issues; integrate compliance into what you're doing now so that it integrates into the everyday business of the organization.

Training Adult Learners

- Acknowledge "life learning"
- Acknowledge self-worth
- Associate the unfamiliar with the familiar
- Recognize individual resourcefulness
- Treat others with respect

- Teach to all types of adult learning styles
    - Auditory learners (use active repetition, songs, skits, et cetera)
    - Visual learners (use handouts, videos, PowerPoint presentations, et cetera)
    - Kinesthetic learners (use hands-on projects, role playing, et cetera)
- Use resources wisely
    - Live training may be most effective but unrealistic for very large organizations
    - Online training courses may not be perfectly tailored to an organization but may still convey the general compliance concepts appropriately, track who has and has not been trained, and use resources more efficiently—consider interactive scenarios for online training
    - Provide longer, more intensive training sessions to employees in certain areas of responsibility and more general compliance training to all other employees
- Use real-life examples from employees' own work—you may want to not refer to specific people or identifying remarks so as not to embarrass anyone, but using examples from employees' actual work will provide for more practical learning and will be more effective. Of course, the more practical and applicable the examples are to the organization's environment, the better.

Should compliance education be voluntary, or mandatory? For general training, every employee, or those who do work on behalf of the organizations, e.g., brokers, contractors, distributors, etc., should be required to sign and date a statement that confirms his or her knowledge of and commitment to the standards of conduct. This attestation should be retained, where appropriate.

> ### Sample Attestation/Acknowledgement Form
>
> This is to acknowledge that I have received and reviewed Our Organization's Code of Conduct. I agree to comply with the standards contained in the code and all related policies and procedures as is expected as part of my continued employment or association with the organization. I acknowledge that the code is only a statement of principles for individual and business conduct and does not constitute an employment contract. I will report any potential violation of which I become aware promptly to my supervisor or the compliance officer. I understand that any violation of the code of conduct or any organization policy or procedure is grounds for disciplinary action, up to and including discharge from employment (or language similar regarding country-specific laws).
>
> _____   _____
> Date   Name (Please Print) / Signature

It should be clear by now that compliance cannot be a one-time educational event. Your compliance committee can help in assessing the best approach on such issues as whether to make education mandatory or voluntary and how to structure education and training options within the organization. Again, your organization's culture is the driving force. Education and training are your best strategies for prevention. Remember to attend to your own educational needs as well. The more you know, the better you can identify and meet the educational needs of staff.

4. Monitoring and Auditing

Before you begin the auditing and monitoring process, you must understand the difference between auditing and monitoring. Auditing is viewed as a formalized method for the audit process (define review scope, develop review criteria, identify sampling methodology and select sample, conduct review, document findings, and follow up on management action plans to assure observations are resolved). Auditing is independent of management, without any real and/or potential vested interest in the outcome.

Monitoring is a day to day process and commonly used by management to assist them to identify how operational aspects of compliance might be occurring. Monitoring does not have to be independent, but can be. Independence is an important concept in auditing because it is key for the compliance function in providing objective assurance to the board/and others. It is an effective way to ensure that management has resolved issues identified and has implemented appropriate systems and controls to mitigate and/or eliminate risks and to prevent reoccurrence of the risk. To develop an auditing and monitoring plan, the compliance officer must conduct a risk assessment to identify, analyze and prioritize the risks that should be included in the plan. The plan should be dynamic and constantly evaluated to assure that it is meeting the priorities of the organization related to compliance risks. If the compliance department is covering only a single area of compliance, e.g., financial, FCPA, etc., then it is important that communication and integration of all compliance risks be integrated into a comprehensive, enterprise-wide compliance risk-based plan. This will allow an organization to view, at a glance, its overall compliance auditing and monitoring plan, and to identify whether the plan is duplicative and available resources are utilized efficiently and effectively. This type of focus will also assist in assuring the most appropriate subject matter experts are available for these activities, which will increase credibility and outcomes. Auditing and monitoring usually evolves with the compliance program's maturity. No one can expect 100 percent compliance from the first day. The key is to strive for and demonstrate a process for continually improving upon compliance activities. The goal of evaluation is to assess, at least annually, the priority risks of the organization.

Best practice is for the compliance audit and monitoring plan to focus on the prioritized risks of the organization; i.e., to develop a risk-based plan. There are certain functions common to all types of organizations that should be reviewed:

- Third party intermediaries or improper business relationship issues
- Conflicts of interest
- Intellectual property
- Data privacy and security
- Foreign corrupt practices

- Antitrust
- Contract management, i.e.: appropriateness and compliance with contract terms
- Travel and entertainment
- Compliance program processes and effectiveness
- Other functions (this will depend on the type of organization).

For example, publicly traded companies should have their financial statements and supporting worksheets audited regularly. Compliance may assist an interval audit function or be the primary auditor for this area if that department is responsible for compliance with laws such as, in the United States, the Sarbanes-Oxley Act and Securities Exchange Commission requirements. Not-for-profit organizations are also accountable for aspects similar to those of publicly traded companies. They must demonstrate accountability and responsibility for accuracy of funds and disclosures of material weaknesses in controls or material financial losses. In the United States, these requirements are identified through different state and federal requirements. Efforts in the auditing of financial statements again would be most effective when integrated into an overall comprehensive compliance risk plan for the organization. Any areas of concern previously identified either internally or by an outside agency should be looked at carefully and regularly.

There are at least two ways to approach auditing, the concurrent or the retrospective audit. Every organization is unique, and, again, you must do what is best for your organization and what is more appropriate for the specific situation. Regardless of the method, it is important to understand the pros and cons of each. For instance, retrospective is often utilized because information is more easily obtained for the sampling process. Forensic capabilities are enhanced with retrospective sampling because the sample usually is more complete. However, it is important to develop a milestone as to the timeframe to which you go back; i.e., new process was developed, new system or new product added, change in policy or law, etc. This will assist in defining the "why" of that chosen timeframe if you should have to defend your approach with any internal or external inquiry.

A retrospective audit will provide a baseline risk assessment, or a snapshot of where you are—in a specific risk process area. It is, at best, optimistic to think that one can identify in some finite period of time everything that could possibly be wrong and then try to set up a realistic timeframe for addressing those problems. Moreover, any problems identified in a retrospective audit will require not only corrective actions to ensure the problem does not recur, but also remedies to any third parties who may have been affected. It is an organization's duty as part of its compliance program to remediate any problems identified. Thus, they cannot merely "go forward" after a retrospective audit has identified past improprieties, which again is why a milestone for a timeframe of the audit is critical.

A concurrent audit will identify and address potential problems individually as they arise and before they cause harm to another party. If a problem does indeed exist, then steps can be taken to correct the related process and any policies or procedures that reflect the process. Once the change has been communicated to all affected parties, then those in charge of the audit can go back in a predetermined amount of time (e.g., three months and perhaps again in six months) to review the process and resulting documents to ensure that the problem has been resolved. It may be determined upon repeated review that further corrective actions may be necessary, including disciplinary action against employees who continually fail to correct the problem after repeated retraining. Concurrent auditing is the preferred method for helping to change behavior, as the individual is in "real time" and can quickly make changes to be compliant. Retrospective observations (in the past), are harder to use for reinforcing behavior changes, because by the time it is communicated to the appropriate party, the information is "old."

It is possible to be effective in auditing and monitoring by using both approaches—a retrospective audit to get a baseline comparison, as well as to identify risks developed due to changes in the systems, regulations, etc.; and a concurrent audit to get a "real time" comparison.

There are various approaches to sampling for auditing and monitoring. Considerations include the overall purpose of the auditing and monitoring activity, where the results will ultimately be reported (internal or external), and the approach (retrospective or concurrent). Statistically valid sampling is the most credible for identifying the risk problem. However, this approach is resource intensive and requires expertise in defining the statistically valid sample. Other types of sampling that are not statistically valid are also available and tend to be more commonly utilized due to resource limitations and other variables. It is important to note that statistically valid sampling is the only method that allows the findings to be applied to the whole population being looked at and not just the sample population. Whereas, any other type of sampling will only apply to the sample itself, not the whole population.

Monitoring, or regular review, is also necessary to determine whether compliance elements, such as dissemination of standards, training, and disciplinary action, have been satisfied. This method also will target potential deficiencies and areas where modifications might be in order. A good place to begin an internal assessment is by interviewing employees. Employees have a wealth of knowledge, and perhaps surprisingly, they often enjoy participating in the process of improving the organization for which they work. Thus, they will offer an unexpected amount of information. Ask them openly about risk, about their daily activities, the processes, procedures, and the soundness of each. Ask if the policies and procedures are followed. Periodically send out questionnaires to staff for feedback, or conduct focus groups. Remember to always reassure employees that the organization maintains a strict non-retaliation policy—that employees will not be retaliated against for reporting suspected misconduct.

Set up systems for regular and sometimes random review of records, both final documents (e.g., invoices, financial statements) and supporting documents (e.g., invoices, worksheets, notes, legal opinions, financial analyses, schedules, budgets, expenses). Data collection and tracking are the heart and soul of review because they provide trend analysis and a measure of progress. The compliance officer or reviewer should consider the following techniques:

- Onsite visits
- Interviews with personnel involved in management, operations, legal, procurement, marketing, finance, and other related activities
- Questionnaires developed to solicit impressions of a broad cross-section of the organization's employees and staff
- Reviews of written materials and documentation prepared by the different business units of the organization

- Trend analyses or longitudinal studies that seek deviations, positive or negative, in specific areas over a given period
- Review of internal and external complaints filed
- At performance review time, interviews should question if there are any areas of potential wrongdoing or noncompliance to be aware of. This approach provides another avenue for employees to raise an issue.
- Pose compliance-related questions in exit interviews to identify potential risks.

Sample Compliance-Related Exit Interview Questions

Responses to these questions should be reported to the compliance officer:

- How do you think the organization lives up to its code of conduct?
- Did you have any concerns about ethical issues or compliance-related practices? If so, please explain.
- Did you have any hesitation in raising any issues – in your chain of command?
- Would you go around your chain of command if there were areas you felt weren't being addressed?

(*See Appendix A.5, Sample Audit Review Form.*)

Who is responsible for coordinating the monitoring, for conducting the internal audit? Is this an internal auditor's responsibility, the compliance office's responsibility, or perhaps a combination of the two? First, to avoid duplication or overlap, consider if there are other departments in your organization performing audits. Quality improvement or quality assurance activities are usually underway at all levels of the organization. Additionally, the nomenclature for these activities may have a different definition for their "auditing and monitoring" activity than for those done by the compliance department. It will be important organization-wide that your definitions are in sync and that you can leverage these departments' activities for your compliance auditing and monitoring plan. They will dovetail with the monitoring and auditing elements of an effective compliance program. Auditors will need experience in the area they are observing. Consider internal ad hoc groups—compliance swat teams that include subject matter experts—to monitor specific issues or review potential problem areas. References should be carefully checked for any outside auditors employed by the organization.

An important concept for the auditing and monitoring plan is that it is dynamic and should be periodically reviewed with senior leadership to determine if the priorities identified are still the priorities of the organization. Examples of plan templates are provided in Appendix A.9, Audit Review Plan Templates.

Any questions posed to, or communications with, government, regulatory agencies, or industry associations will be taken into account in an audit or a monitoring effort. The larger your organization, the greater the difficulty will be in documenting such contacts. Be sure to take notes when you have a telephone conversation with the government or other regulatory agency, ask for written confirmation of the information provided, but always keep your own notes of the conversation, including the date, time, and contact name as well as the specifics of the conversation. As a preventive measure, in some instances, it might be useful to meet periodically with a regulatory representative to discuss industry issues as well as specific questions you may have. Such meetings build better communication lines and enhance understanding of expectations and requirements.

Auditing and monitoring activity must be documented to demonstrate overall attention to real and/or potential compliance risks. The plan, observations, action plans and resolution of issues should be regularly reported to senior company officers as appropriate. Additionally, results from an ongoing evaluation of the compliance program should be reported to the senior leader (e.g. CEO, president), governing body, and members of the compliance committee no less than annually. Monitoring and auditing activities should be a key feature of any annual review.

Reports to management, the governing body, and the compliance committee should include findings or suspicions of misconduct with an action plan to address and resolve the potential problem.

5. Reporting and Investigating

A positive cultural tone is critical for being successful in encouraging employees to voluntarily report issues. There are a variety of methods for employees to report potential problems or to raise concerns. Some of these will be dependent on country-specific laws for establishing reporting mechanisms; i.e., the French data protection laws, etc. Communication is very important in the compliance process. The most important reporting system is an open door, and the best reporting system is one where the employee feels comfortable approaching his or her supervisor and openly discussing any potential problem.

For any reporting method to be effective, employees must accept that there will be no retaliation or retribution for coming forward. Again, emphasis in the cultural tone will help an employee be encouraged to report, or it may actually have a negative influence on reporting if the tone is one of subtle or overt retaliation being supported. The concept of non-retaliation is fundamental to the compliance program, and a clearly stated policy regarding non-retribution is the first step. (*See Appendix A.2 Sample Non-retaliation/Non-retribution Policy.*) The dangers are real. If employees suspect there could be retaliation, no one will come forward, creating fertile ground for whistleblowers and exposing the organization to unchecked risk.

Confidentiality is also key. Policies and procedures should assure confidentiality and anonymity to the extent possible in all reporting processes. (*See Appendix A.6, Sample Confidentiality Statement.*) Confidentiality is, of course, closely tied with non-retaliation. For example, the decision-making process regarding a promotion can be tainted if the supervisor has been informed of an employee-candidate's report of a problem. Policies and procedures need to offer assurances to the employee but also must note that resolution of a problem, which could include legal action, may in certain circumstances require disclosure of identity. Legal counsel should review both the non-retaliation and confidentiality policies to be sure unrealistic promises are not made.

One common reporting method recommended is the hotline or helpline. Again, some countries have limitations, or do not allow the use of this method. There are various arguments for whether to handle a hotline internally or externally. The size and setting of the organization must factor into the decision. A large organization may need 24-hour coverage. For a smaller organization, 24-hour coverage may not be needed or may only be feasible through outsourcing. Either way, cost and/or resources are a consideration here. If you decide to outsource, the contract should include the following:

- the right to move the toll-free number to another vendor or bring it in-house
- assurances that security of the vendor's computer system equals the security provided for the data within your own system
- the ability for case management of the calls
- the ability for analytics and reports to assist you in identifying trends, outliers, etc.

Whether you handle your hotline internally or whether you outsource, anonymity must be promised to the extent possible. All country specific laws should be taken into consideration. Hotline numbers and procedures must be clearly and readily communicated to staff, preferably not solely through a page in the employee policies and procedures manual. Requirements to post the number may exist for certain rules/laws in some countries. Ongoing communication, regardless of the reporting method, should include encouraging and instilling the responsibility of each individual employee to report any issues, and to understand how to report a problem or a question.

Once you have established how to report issues, how do you assess effectiveness? Does frequency of issues reported necessarily indicate that employees know and understand their duty to report issues or that your method of reporting is working? Not necessarily. If you have been able to create an environment and culture where issues are raised through appropriate channels, where staff trusts they can report problems without fear of retaliation, you may not get a lot of calls. Industry, generally, has identified that approximately 80 percent of hotline calls in the first year are human resources or employer-employee relations issues—complaints about a supervisor's behavior or a colleague's allegedly insulting remark, or disagreements with the organization's policy on work hours for example. Over time, these types of calls may decrease, but the trend tends to be that 40% to 60% of calls remain that way after the initial period of implementation. Here again, consider your organization's culture. The number of calls alone, however, is not an indicator of effectiveness.

In addition to a reporting mechanism like a hotline, some organizations have in-house e-mail systems. E-mail can be configured so that problems can be reported, but the compliance officer cannot determine who is sending the e-mail. In today's work environment, computers are commonplace, but they are not ubiquitous. Some jobs do not require a desk with access to a computer, and a centrally located general-access terminal could compromise confidentiality. For these reasons, e-mail probably shouldn't be the only reporting system. If adopting this sort of system as part of your reporting options, however, remember to emphasize in your procedures that anyone who does want to hear back will need to include his or her name in the body of the e-mail since there will be no way for the compliance officer to know who sent the e-mail.

Another reporting option is a drop box, a variation on the old suggestion box. Regular and frequent pick-ups will be important, and multiple locations are encouraged—although be sure not to position any in an area of the institution with a security camera.

Reporting works both ways, of course, and the compliance officer should take every opportunity to keep in touch with all levels of staff. Regular ongoing communication is another form of education that reiterates commitment and can facilitate prevention of problems. Compliance communication can be incorporated into existing systems—a compliance column of frequently asked questions in the organization's in-house newsletter, posters on bulletin boards and periodic compliance blasts through news flashes. Good channels for communication must be in place and effective when changes to policy, special alerts or settlements occur that you want to make known quickly to a select employee population. Whatever communication you choose to use, be sure to keep copies in a binder or file so you can document what you are communicating, how, to whom, and when. All-staff e-mails, articles in the in-house newsletter, a page on the company Intranet, brief presentations at all staff meetings—all these methods of communication will reinforce the visibility of the compliance department and its availability to staff.

Once a complaint is received or a question is raised, what should happen next must be pre-determined. The process for handling complaints or questions should be defined so that the caller will know at a high level what to expect. There should be a method of determining if the matter needs a simple answer by management, needs further investigation, or lacks enough information to identify next steps. Sometimes issues come forward without enough information; your process should have a way to reach out to the complainant to ask further questions, e.g., web access, e-mail, etc. The process for how calls or input to the reporting mechanism will be addressed should be written in your policy and procedures. Specific steps for an investigation should be enumerated, and such a policy must limit distribution of information to protect confidentiality and non-retaliation commitments. Formal reporting mechanisms can seem like a sizeable expense, but in many if not most organizations, they are a practical investment. The employee's options shouldn't be limited to regulator-sponsored hotlines.

While carrying out an investigation, documentation is everything. All complaints must be logged and tracked. Many organizations assign a unique number to each call so that the caller can check on the status of the complaint by calling back and giving the assigned number. How the complaint was handled, by whom, and when should all be included in the documentation. (*See Appendix A.7, Sample Complaint Information Sheet.*) The detail of the concern needs to be documented but may reside in another file, department, etc. Documentation of the specifics of the issue, the departments involved, findings, and actions taken is necessary. (*See Appendix A.8, Sample Compliance Issue Follow-Up Form.*) You also need a clearly stated procedure outlining the disposition of these forms; specifically, who gets copies and how information is incorporated into written reports. All written reports of investigations should be consistent in format and in procedures for how and to whom the report will be disseminated.

It is important to note that workplace investigations require a specific skill set. If an investigations team is selected, make sure they get the proper training on how to conduct investigations and how to determine appropriate subject matter experts to include. Where appropriate, legal should be consulted in regards to process and documentation. In addition, where applicable, procedures should detail how to determine whether an attorney-directed investigation would result in a better outcome.

6. Enforcement and Discipline

Fair, equitable, and consistent are the watchwords for enforcing the standards of conduct and the policies and procedures. The place to start with enforcement is back at the beginning with the standards of conduct and the policies and procedures. The organization's compliance and ethics program should be promoted and enforced consistently throughout the organization. To accomplish this goal, enforcement and discipline should include appropriate incentives to perform in accordance with the compliance and ethics program, and appropriate disciplinary measures for engaging in criminal conduct and for failing to take reasonable steps to prevent or detect criminal conduct. These disciplinary measures should be spelled out in a written policy statement and consistent with any other policies and procedures on discipline that might exist in the organization. Country specific laws/regulations, i.e., work council, labor laws, union, etc. should be considered in this element.

The policy's content may cover areas such as:

- Noncompliance will be punished
- Failure to report noncompliance will be punished
- An outlined set of disciplinary procedures will be followed (unless defined in another policy, in which case that should be referenced)
- The parties responsible for appropriate action
- A promise that discipline will be fair and consistent.

It is important to emphasize that "sins of omission" as well as "sins of commission" will be subject to discipline. Failure to detect or report an offense is a serious act of noncompliance and equally as deserving of discipline as the actual misconduct. Compliance is an active, ongoing process that is everyone's responsibility.

In this area, consultations with the organization's human resources (HR) department would be important. There are no doubt disciplinary policies and procedures already in place with which you will need to be consistent, and which can serve as a model. One important piece of advice your HR colleagues will probably give you is that you cannot discipline without having properly informed all employees of the rules. Although stated earlier, it bears reiteration here too—the policies and procedures must be clear, and they must be appropriately communicated to all staff. It is much more difficult to penalize someone for violating a policy he or she did not know about. Hence, the first step toward enforcement is distributing standards of conduct and policies and procedures and educating staff about them, including the consequences of noncompliance.

Written standards of conduct are important, so that you can address the procedures for handling disciplinary problems and those who will be responsible for taking appropriate action. Depending on the country you work in, intentional or reckless noncompliance may be punishable with significant sanctions, which can range from oral warnings to suspension, privilege revocation (subject to any applicable peer review procedures), termination, or financial penalties as appropriate. Many organizations use progressive discipline. As the name implies, this is a multi-step process where the penalties become increasingly more severe. The first step in this process may be defined by specific country labor laws, but minimally, the supervisor should meet with the employee to secure the employee's understanding of the problem and a commitment to correcting the inappropriate behavior. Depending on the situation, the next step may again be defined by country-specific labor laws, which is why any discipline should be done by management in consultation with HR. Subsequent steps might include suspension without pay or infliction of a probationary period where the employee is advised to correct the behavior within a certain time period, say 30 days, or face termination. The final step is termination once all other options have been exhausted. The severity of the infraction will determine the steps. Certainly, this discussion can assist the supervisor in identifying employee understanding of the issue. The basic supervisor's discussion does not require an excessive process. Documentation of the process and discussion will be essential.

If there are no other requirements defined, then a typical disciplinary action chain would include the following (the steps may be repeated more than once or skipped depending on level and intentionality of offense):

- Verbal warning
- Written warning
- Suspension
- Fine(s)
- Termination.

Punishment should be commensurate with the offense. There are offenses, such as blatant acts of fraud, that warrant immediate termination, but most infractions will be relatively minor and most likely unintentional. These may best be handled with education or additional training. Education should never be labeled as "punishment." When put in a positive and supportive context, it can efficiently correct noncompliant behavior. Be sure your policies and procedures include remedial steps such as additional training.

Background checks including references are encouraged, where possible, for all new employees. If there are no legal and/or regulatory restraints on conducting background checks, an organization should consider when and how to periodically do background checks on current employees; i.e., at promotion, regularly required because of the type of business, etc.

This proactive strategy can prevent hiring a sanctioned individual (which itself may be prohibited by a government entity). Such cautions apply to contracts with outside vendors as well. All are acting as agents of your organization, and due diligence is needed to assure you have "good faith citizens" working for the organization.

Enforcement is not just about discipline, of course. Goals and objectives for individuals and departments can include specific references to compliance. Achievement of those goals, especially when celebrated, is a positive reinforcement that encourages support for and enforcement of the compliance program. Performance appraisals need not focus solely on issues of noncompliance. They can, for example, make note of favorable or improved audit or monitoring outcomes. Your compliance program can be better enforced if you also find ways to reinforce with positive feedback.

7. Response and Prevention

If there should ever be reason to believe that misconduct or wrongdoing has actually occurred, the organization must respond appropriately. Failure to respond or to engage in lengthy delay can have serious consequences. Violations of the compliance program and other types of misconduct threaten an organization's status as reliable, honest, and trustworthy. Detected but uncorrected misconduct can seriously endanger the mission, reputation, and legal status of the organization. Ignoring a legitimate report of wrongdoing also will alienate staff, especially the person who reported the problem, and hence encourage whistleblower action. Cover-ups usually cause more problems than they solve. In the event of misconduct, face the problem and fix it. However daunting it may feel to be faced with the possibility of misconduct, remember that one of the goals of a compliance program is *detection*. Having found a problem is an indication your program is working.

The first logical step is to meet with your in-house or external legal counsel. Together you can determine how serious the misconduct or wrongdoing is and develop an appropriate plan of action. It is recommended that an investigation be done any time a potential violation is identified. Therefore, your plan of action will likely begin with a thorough *internal investigation*. Depending on the extent and seriousness of the alleged infraction, outside counsel or content experts may be needed. Your counsel will help decide what protections, if any, can be used in the investigation. While an internal investigation is the first step, also be sure to take the necessary steps immediately to stop or modify the procedures that are the alleged source of wrongdoing.

The internal investigation must be handled carefully and documented meticulously. When choosing an investigative team, look for those who are knowledgeable about the area in question but who are also capable of being objective. The compliance officer obviously should be a part of the team, but to emphasize commitment, participation by a member of the senior staff is desirable when possible. If outside consultants are used, the compliance office still must be represented on the team. Handing the problem off to someone else is not a solution. Outside consultants will need to be directed, overseen, and evaluated just as closely as an internal investigation team, if not more so. The team should meet together as a group in the beginning to delineate the problem, decide on an approach or strategy, and get the guidance and support of senior management. Instructions on timeframe, process, and the need for documentation are also in order. At minimum, the team should meet together again as a group at the end of the investigative process to discuss findings and plan the final report. Time is of the essence. Prompt reporting of misconduct to the appropriate regulatory authority within a reasonable period needs to occur, when applicable, after determining that there is credible evidence of a violation. Timely reporting may help to avoid fines and penalties.

As noted above, detailed documentation is critical. If it should be necessary to defend the actions of the organization, a clear paper trail will make the process much easier. Thorough documentation will include the following:

- Description of the potential misconduct and how it was reported
- Description of the investigative process
- List of relevant documents reviewed
- List of employees interviewed

- Employee interview questions and notes as determined by the organization
- Changes to policies and procedures, if appropriate
- Documentation of any disciplinary actions—if appropriate; sometimes these actions are documented separately
- Investigation final report with recommended remedial actions.

The final report and any attached documentation are sensitive materials and should be distributed in limited quantities.

If the investigation finds that there was no violation, it should be documented that the allegation was unsubstantiated. However, if, after the internal investigation, there is reason to believe the organization's misconduct constituted a material violation of the law, then the organization must take steps to disclose the violation to the appropriate regulatory agency.

Voluntary disclosure to a regulatory agency should be a consideration to demonstrate the organization's willingness to be transparent in areas within which they have had wrongdoing. It may also provide certain financial advantages, if disclosure results in fines being reduced, or certain administrative advantages, if a good faith effort to comply creates a more pleasant working relationship between the organization and the investigators.

Organizations are expected to police themselves and work with external regulatory agencies to correct problems. Sometimes, by self-reporting, the organization may have the option of conducting a self-audit (following regulatory guidelines) rather than an imposed regulatory audit. Such a self-audit would communicate the scope of the problem in the following ways:

- **What is the origin of the issue?** An accounting concern may be the result of a systematic practice, a third-party inquiry, or misconduct by individuals. A systematic noncompliant accounting practice may have been tied to a new system implementation or the result of faulty advice received from a consultant, for example.

- **When did the issue originate?** A systematic accounting practice may warrant internal inquiry into the origin of the practice and the extent of its impact on the organization. Improper accounting methods by one individual may require scrutiny of his or her entire employment history as well as a review of directions that person may have received from management.

- **How far back should the investigation go?** Investigation standards for one organization may not apply to another. Some will begin by reviewing the past year's accounting records. Others may start with a month of prior records. Regardless of the methods used, key stakeholders must determine the parameters of its investigation based on a reasonable approach that is justified under the circumstances.

- **Can extrapolation of a statistical sample be used?** Statistical sampling and extrapolation may be warranted for some investigations. Caution should be used in that the sample may not accurately represent an organization's entire population of the factor being investigated.

Understood, of course, is that any identified problem must be corrected immediately. Restitution if applicable, should be prompt, and when the problem is rectified, the issue should be added to the list of topics to be addressed with regular internal monitoring.

It is also possible that a regulatory agency could approach the organization with information about an alleged violation; investigating a charge of fraud related to business contracted with a branch of government, for example. In such an instance the agency may send official representatives to the organization to conduct the internal investigation. If this happens, rumors and speculations will run rampant. It will be especially important to keep staff informed about what is going on. To get the message to employees, consider different options for the appropriate method of communication. For example,

- The president or high-ranking administrator should send an all-staff memo or e-mail
- Hold an all-staff meeting to get the word out and answer questions
- Keep managers and department heads updated so they can "drill down" the message

- Provide opportunities for feedback and more questions from staff.

Most important, the organization's policies and procedures should include instructions for employees on what to expect and how to handle contact from an outside regulatory agency about an investigation. Legal counsel must be actively involved in the drafting of these policies. In the event of an onsite regulatory agency investigation, legal counsel must be notified immediately. Any documents presented by the outside agency should be reviewed carefully to ensure only identified documents are provided for the investigation matter they have defined. Also, the compliance officer should be present during the investigation, keeping a detailed, written account of all activities and an itemized inventory of documents inspected or removed from the premises.

3

Organizational Steps

1. Gain Support and Commitment

Board of Directors or Governing Committee Support

Compliance begins with the governing board. Support from the top is very important; there can be no program at all, much less an effective one, without the vision and guidance of the board. It is the board that officially recognizes the need for a compliance program and authorizes its launch and implementation, including the hiring of a compliance officer. The first step toward implementation of a compliance plan is management's communication of its commitment. A resolution or memo from the board stating its unequivocal support for the program is a strong beginning. *(See Appendix A.10 Sample Board of Directors Resolution.)* The source of such a statement may be different depending on the organization. In some organizations it might come from the chairman of the board, in others from the CEO. Whatever the source, board endorsement must be in a written format; it must communicate unqualified support for and commitment to the compliance process and ethical business behavior; and it must be effectively communicated to everyone.

One option is for the chairman of the board, CEO, or president to distribute the memo or resolution to all business unit leaders. The business unit leader then distributes the document to managers so that the word trickles down and the message is reinforced that all managers endorse the compliance program. This approach also makes the compliance program directly accessible to staff and gives staff an opportunity to discuss the document in relatively small groups. A special department or unit meeting to discuss the program and distribute the letter can lend weight to the message, or it can be an agenda item for a regularly scheduled meeting. Whatever the venue, staff should be given ample opportunity to ask questions and offer feedback.

Moreover, the board's role does not end with voting to establish a compliance program and distributing a letter of support—nor does its responsibility. Ongoing, visible support from the board of directors is crucial. Most people care about what the boss cares about. When the board takes compliance seriously, that sense of importance will trickle down. Your board may need guidance in understanding the seriousness of compliance. They may not immediately recognize that "doing the right thing" adds up to good business and that compliance is a good, long-term investment. The board of directors or governing committee, meeting infrequently and not always aware of day-to-day operations, can be insulated from problems. In the case of compliance, however, the board must understand the implications of not taking active measures to prevent potential wrongdoing. They should be educated about the potential for liability and reminded of the U.S. Caremark International Derivative Litigation (though U.S.-oriented, the governance principles are applicable to most organizations), which makes the board responsible for implementation of a system to gather information on the company's efforts to prevent and detect fraud and abuse. It is in the best interest of the organization to have the board take an active rather than a passive role in compliance.

Support from Management

Management plays an influencing role in making compliance work with support expressed in a myriad of ways. Attendance at educational programs cannot be mandatory for everyone except managers and vice presidents. Making time to demonstrate a personal commitment goes a long way to enhancing a system-wide commitment. After attending training sessions, managers should discuss the content with staff either at a regular department meeting or as circumstances permit, one-on-one.

Supervisors or managers also must lead by example, for actions speak louder than words. A manager cannot encourage employees to report questionable behavior and then give special treatment to a friend. Once a potential infraction is reported, the non-retaliation policy must be rigorously observed. It is up to management to make sure employees do not hesitate to come forward for fear of retaliation.

"Tone in the middle" is also very important for an organization's culture. While the top leaders may be supporting the compliance efforts, if there is no follow through and incentives built in for middle management, the culture will fail in its efforts for an effective compliance program.

Staying on top of compliance issues is a manager's day-to-day obligation. Managers and supervisors must closely follow news and information from their professional organizations and pass along any and all compliance-related issues to the compliance office. The compliance officer is encouraged to be proactive and, from time to time, to ask managers and supervisors what new regulations are developing in their fields.

Support from Professionals

Certain industries revolve around key professionals who hold influential positions in the organization. Examples of key professionals in select industries include physicians in health care, engineers in building, attorneys in legal, programmers in computer science, investigators in research, et cetera. These individuals play key leadership roles in their industries. Frequent situations will arise where one of these individual's support can make all the difference in creating a true culture of compliance. It is thus to your advantage to find a key professional champion—someone who understands and supports the mission of the compliance program and who will back you up when needed. Moreover, this professional can be a model of how employees can effectively incorporate compliance into their other job functions without distracting from the performance of their actual duties and without consuming inordinate and unacceptable amounts of time. This key professional can advocate compliance in several ways:

- Emphasize operational and fiscal improvements gained through compliance
- Provide data to support compliance activities and improvements
- Build trust through involvement
- Be a partner, not a dictator

- Cultivate the early adopters and enthusiasts
- Communicate, communicate, communicate.

The earlier you achieve professional buy-in the better. Invite professionals to compliance implementation committee meetings and actively seek their input throughout the start-up—and beyond. Many organizations have a strong professional presence on their compliance committees. If at all possible, consider having a professional chair the compliance committee. When funding permits, sending a key professional to a compliance conference can provide valuable education as well as increased awareness and additional support. Achieving professional buy-in will be an important challenge, but it is a critical element of launching an effective compliance program.

Support from Staff

It isn't a crime to make a mistake; it is a crime not to do anything about the mistake once it is detected. In launching a compliance program, staff will need to be convinced that looking for problem areas is not the sole responsibility of the compliance office—it is everyone's job. Education is the first step to take, but also look for ways to heighten awareness on a day-to-day basis. When launching a compliance program, some organizations will distribute cups or pens with a compliance slogan and the organization name or logo. Everybody loves something for free, and if the budget permits, these items can increase awareness and foster cooperation.

Staff buy-in will correlate directly with the organization's ability to foster an environment of trust. As emphasized earlier, accepting the non-retaliation policy will be the best way to ensure active staff participation. Rewarding and thanking those who come forward to report an issue will provide immediate positive feedback to staff and will offer a long-term reward for the compliance program overall.

2. Establish Financial Support

Management, up to and including the board of directors, also must be willing to make a financial commitment to compliance. Resources and space cost money, and most organizations have limited, even diminishing resources.

While the level of commitment is not necessarily correlated directly with the resources (human and financial) allocated, a reasonable budget must be developed in consultation with the compliance officer. An organization unwilling to commit the necessary resources isn't demonstrating support for the compliance program and—unquestionably and unfortunately—that message too will filter down through the organization.

Compliance Budget

Knowing what to do won't make it happen. The reality is you can't do it without money. But how much money will be required? The right amount will depend on the organization, its size, and scope. Remember, the compliance program must influence everyone in the organization; adequate funding will go a long way in demonstrating and eliciting commitment. This is a good place to mention again that the only thing worse than having no policies is having them and not following them. Under-funding can be one source of such a situation. If investigated, a compliance program's value in any settlement will depend largely on the regulatory agency's interpretation of the organization's commitment to good corporate citizenship. In fact, "a compliance program that has neither the moral nor the budgetary support of senior management may actually be deemed as tacit approval for the inappropriate activities."[5]

Both external and internal risks and the controls to manage those risks factor into a budget. An identified risk area may require immediate attention and hence extra expense, perhaps specialized training or a new computer software program. Bear in mind that certain internal factors can impact, directly or indirectly, the compliance budget. For instance, if your organization has a high turnover rate, the compliance budget will need to provide for training the flow of new employees as well as the existing staff. A highly decentralized operation may call for either a centralization compliance process or additional monitoring to ensure procedures are consistent or at least consistently enforced. Other factors that can impact the compliance budget are poor communications infrastructure, poor data processing controls, and compensation structures that emphasize financial performance with no compliance considerations.

Staffing

Organization size, setting, and culture will influence how the compliance department is staffed. In some organizations the compliance officer role may not be full time, but rather a fraction of a full-time equivalent (FTE) position. In a large, multi-site location, the compliance department will be much more extensive. There are a variety of staffing possibilities for a compliance department. An education coordinator can make a vital contribution to a program's effort, because a large amount of employee education needs to be conducted. Other valuable positions include someone to accumulate and analyze compliance data and an auditor who can regularly audit or monitor and help with documentation. Secretarial or administrative support also is helpful. If you are unable to add these resources to your staffing contingency, identify where in your organization you could possibly leverage these types of resources through a shared model—this option may suffice while you are building the program capacity and rationale for the compliance resources ongoing.

For larger organizations considering staffing needs, it will be important for there to be a compliance designate or compliance field liaison who will help facilitate the compliance efforts at remote locations. "Full" or "part-time" compliance personnel will need appropriate training and resources, and this can be provided in many ways on site. Some examples might include a reference binder, a written phone number to call with questions, and focused training on key areas of risk and/or process. Additionally, it can be helpful to involve these individuals in process and approach development so that they will have ownership. Be sure to budget accordingly.

Ongoing Operations

There are other operational expenses to consider, beginning with some sort of reporting method. Reporting mechanisms (e.g., hotlines, e-mails, etc.) can be handled internally or externally; the costs of each option will need to be assessed. Having a mechanism handled externally may be more economically feasible for many organizations. As stated earlier in Chapter 2, considerations regarding any reporting mechanisms must include the country-specific laws or regulations regarding these mechanisms. When looking for outside help, secure competitive bids, and be sure they are based on comparable information. It may be worthwhile to request outside proposals before you make a final decision. There's nothing to lose in finding out what an external resource can do for you.

Educational materials can be a considerable compliance expense. A video program for general sessions and new employee orientation may be helpful. A video customized to your organization can be very expensive, but "off the shelf" videos exist that may well meet your needs. You also will need to provide for specialized training for certain professionals as well as key departments and employees. Such training often is provided through outside consultants or specialists and hence will have budget implications. In-house and ongoing training may require audio-visual equipment and software to create engaging visual materials. There will be costs for printing announcements, agendas, and handouts. Costs for printing the code of conduct and policies and procedures can be a surprisingly large number, and while the code of conduct doesn't need to look like the annual report produced by a marketing company, it deserves a professional and credible look for the organization. Find the right look and feel for your organization—just remember to budget accordingly.

Internet access today is a must. All relevant regulatory documents are available online as are innumerable other helpful compliance-related sites. Adequate computer support is critical.

Professional journals and newsletters are vital ways of keeping abreast of new developments, best practices, and industry trends. They also will provide articles, suggestions, and ideas that can be circulated to appropriate managers or adapted for internal newsletters. Consider budgeting each year for electronic and hardcopy materials so you can gradually build a compliance library that will be a resource for the organization. Also, membership in professional organizations, such as the Society of Corporate Compliance and Ethics (SCCE), is a good investment. Belonging to a professional organization such as SCCE reinforces your professional standing and provides you with a growing network of invaluable resources.

Investigative costs can be unpredictable, especially when an organization is in a state of crisis or turmoil. The compliance office should at least use a comparison from year to year to try to estimate these costs. If the program is new, an estimate of costs could be based on what other departments spent on compliance-related investigations, especially those that relied on the use of outside resources, since a compliance function could have conducted these investigations internally at a comparative savings.

Finally, if your organization has an in-house counsel, consult with him or her to determine budgetary needs. If you currently rely on external counsel, you may want to alert the firm of your new or expanding compliance program and solicit estimates for additional costs. Such expenses may be part of the legal budget, but it is best to be sure they are appropriately covered somewhere.

Six Tips for Saving on Future Costs of Compliance

1. **Embed quality into existing processes**—If processes that pose the greatest risk to the organization are revisited with an emphasis on quality, then the outcome of this exercise will be increased efficiency, increased customer satisfaction, and better, less expensive compliance.

2. **Centralize common processes and controls where it makes sense**—Scattered efforts could lead to redundancy and inadequate oversight as well as extra expense, if the same functions are being handled within many different departments, e.g., education.

3. **Focus on corporate culture**—This is critical to success and efficiency. Employee satisfaction and retention are good indicators of culture, and employee turnover can be costly to an organization, not only in recruitment efforts, but also in training the new employee.

4. **Improve information system processes**—It is important and cost effective to embed compliance into technology through controls such as edit checks and reports that facilitate monitoring. Efficient technology frees up resources to be used in other areas.

5. **Emphasize training**—The best way to correct an error is to prevent its occurrence. The number one reason people are non-compliant is because they did not know or understand the area of compliance involved.

6. **Monitor marketing and compensation**—Review marketing materials to be certain the message is consistent with corporate philosophy; new business ventures should be evaluated for risk and the ability of the organization to manage the risk; compensation structures should embed measurable compliance objectives.

3. Develop a Code of Conduct

When to roll out your compliance program to staff will depend on many factors. Certainly, the sooner you can enlist staff participation the better, and you need not have everything absolutely final before you officially launch the compliance program companywide. However, you do need to have one of the most important pieces of infrastructure ready and in place as you begin: the organization's code of conduct.

How the code of conduct is written can vary. In some organizations, it is prepared at the board of directors' level. In others it is a compliance officer and/or compliance committee responsibility. If you are in the position of drafting your organization's code of conduct, there are many sources of sample materials. You can look for books with sample codes of conduct included. You could tap into your networking resources to solicit codes of conduct from other organizations. However, it is not advisable to copy a code of conduct from another source, make minor tweaks, and try to make it fit your organization. Your code of conduct should reflect your organization's spirit, tone, and culture. If it isn't culturally acceptable to staff, securing their participation and cooperation in the compliance program will be much more difficult.

There may not be a "one size fits all" code of conduct, but there are certain elements that every code should include. Most codes of conduct begin with the official board of directors' or governing committee's resolution approving the compliance program or the memo announcing the launch of the program. The code should begin with this strong endorsement from the highest levels of management. An endorsement signed by the board chairman or the CEO makes the message personal and says "you have my word on it." This executive message is the place to state unequivocally that everyone in the organization and all affiliates are expected to act in an ethical manner and abide by all applicable laws and regulations affecting the organization. A strong message in support of staff also is in order. The code of conduct provides guidelines and tools developed to help employees in situations created by today's confusing and complex environment. Staff honesty is not the issue. When a situation poses uncertainty, the code of conduct provides guidance for appropriate conduct or, in more challenging situations, offers the way to get answers within the organization.

The code of conduct might be seen as an elaboration on the organization's mission or vision, both of which deserve a highly visible place in the code of conduct. Many organizations have identified specific values that help accomplish the mission. If your organization has values in addition to the mission, these too should be prominently featured in the code of conduct.

As a resource for all staff and affiliates, the code of conduct also should include a detailed outline of procedures for handling questions about compliance or ethical issues, beginning with a description of chain of command. The best reporting mechanism is an open door. When a question arises, it is hoped the employee will feel comfortable in approaching his or her supervisor, the first link in the chain of command. In the event the employee and the supervisor cannot resolve the issue, usually the department manager is the next step. If discussions with the supervisor and department head are not satisfactory, in some organizations the corporate human resources representative is called in. Ultimately, if a compliance-related matter cannot be resolved at the department head or HR level, the corporate compliance officer, who represents executive management, gets involved. These steps should be delineated in the code of conduct along with a clearly stated promise of non-retaliation.

However, every employee will not be comfortable talking to management, so there are alternate methods of reporting potential problems or posing questions. The code of conduct should provide a clear, concise explanation of how those alternate reporting methods work. For instance, where the country-specific laws allow for a hotline reporting mechanism, list the hotline (or helpline) telephone number along with hours of operation. In this context, emphasize that all calls will allow the caller to be anonymous or his or her identity held in complete confidence within the letter of the law. To the extent possible, it will help to outline the procedures for how the organization will respond to reports or questions. Can you promise that the compliance department will investigate all reports? Can you promise that all compliance-related questions or allegations, whether received through chain of command, the hotline, or other reporting mechanism, will be investigated within 48 hours? Such specifics are important to include but will be reassuring to staff only if they are achievable.

As a key element of an effective compliance program, every code of conduct will want to include a description of the resources available to employees if they want to raise an issue. Add phone numbers and e-mail addresses for these contact personnel as well as the compliance officer's contact information.

The narrative section of the code of conduct can deal with a wide variety of issues. For instance, policies on sexual harassment and controlled substances may be addressed. Every code will want to cover expectations regarding conflicts of interest, accepting of gifts and gratuities, protection of intellectual property, and data privacy and security. Areas of specific weakness or risk should be addressed in the code depending on the organization setting. Most importantly, the code must emphasize zero tolerance for fraud or abuse, a commitment to submitting accurate and timely reports to regulatory agencies, and compliance with all laws and regulations. Consequences of malicious or uncorrected wrongdoing should be noted with a description of the progressive discipline procedures, if appropriate. Also, clearly state that everyone has a personal obligation to report any possible wrongdoing. Not reporting makes an employee subject to discipline, too.

The code of conduct holds the potential to be an abstract document, one that might not seem relevant to the day-to-day work of the individual. Therefore, many organizations include a section with frequent scenarios or "examples of compliance violations" to help make the information more practical for the general employee population. A mixture of the general and specific is suggested. Sample general questions might be:

- I think I saw a violation of industry regulations.
  Whom should I contact?
- Should I report a possible problem even if I'm not sure?
  Will I get in trouble?
- What if my supervisor asks me to do something I think is wrong?

- How can I be sure my report will be kept confidential?
- My supervisor is selling tickets to his son's events while at work. Do I have to buy them? Will he be able to retaliate against me if I don't?

Finally, most codes of conduct come with an acknowledgement or attestation form. The attestation form, requiring the employee signature, emphasizes the importance of the document and could provide certain legal advantages should there ever be an outside inquiry. To encourage the employee to return the attestation form promptly, some organizations will require a signed attestation form before new employees can be assigned perquisites such as parking spaces. Attestation forms should be filed in the employee's official human resources file. *(See Chapter 2, No. 3 - Education, for a Sample Attestation Form.)*

4. Identify Staffing Needs

The compliance officer, as noted earlier, is the "focal point" of the compliance program. Education and degree are important considerations in selecting a compliance officer, but more importantly, the position must be filled by someone who will be trusted and well respected within the organization. Background or experience also must be factored in.

All compliance department staff should have job descriptions. If need be, the compliance officer should develop his or her own job description. *(See Appendix A.4, Sample Compliance Officer Job Description.)* Job descriptions for additional department staff should include a detailed list of duties and responsibilities and, to the extent possible, measurable expectations. For an educational coordinator, for example, you might want to require an annual educational plan due by a specific date. An auditor might be expected to review a certain area of risk every month. Job descriptions may need to be modified and adapted as time goes by and as compliance requirements change. Regular employee input to the job description, perhaps in preparation for an annual performance review, will keep the document relevant.

Whatever the size and scope of the organization, all compliance department staff should have certain characteristics. The compliance department is an outreach department, so good "people skills" are vital. There also will be daily interaction with a wide variety of personality types. The ability to stay objective and nonreactive will be an asset to someone working in compliance. Moreover, compliance has a lot to do with change, and in general, people don't like change. Therefore, the compliance staff must from time to time be able to deal with unhappy, dissatisfied staff—especially when delivering difficult news that may mean more work. Strong communication and listening skills will be critical. Discretion also is required. A good sense of humor helps, too. As you interview, probe for these qualities. If you don't find them, keep looking. Once you have staff hired, foster these qualities in them, and provide feedback and guidance in performance reviews.

Most compliance officers would agree that a sizeable majority of compliance activities are related to education and training. Therefore, an education coordinator must be high on the list of early hires. As noted earlier, education is the first and best line of defense in compliance. An educated employee will be less likely to engage in an act of noncompliance and, knowing the organization's commitment to compliance, will be much more likely to come forward if there is a question or concern about potential noncompliance. Having someone to focus on education can make for more and better educational programs and allow the compliance officer to coordinate the big picture. A training coordinator should have a strong background in the industry and solid experience in adult learning strategies. Computer skills are needed not only for PowerPoint presentations, but also for preparing and adapting handouts. Organizational skills are also important; just keeping track of attendance can be a daunting task. Here, too, strong people skills are important.

Monitoring and auditing efforts help ensure that the organization remains vigilant in its compliance efforts. These activities are detective and preventative in nature. Having someone on staff to coordinate these efforts will ensure that regular review happens and that it is objective, documented, reported, and analyzed. This individual also should have specific and high-level experience in the industry, as the complexity of compliance in an organization can only be fully understood by an individual who understands the field. The first step toward prevention is to check competency up front.

5. Conduct Internal Risk Assessment

One of the first steps in launching an effective compliance program is identifying a baseline risk assessment of the operations from a compliance perspective. Establishing baseline information for the compliance officer and other managers helps them to judge progress in reducing or eliminating potential areas of vulnerability. The baseline risk assessment has at least four main objectives. First, it *outlines the current operational standards* of the organization and the extent to which legal requirements are being met. Second, it *identifies real and potential weaknesses*, especially for those procedures used to measure and enforce compliance with legal and regulatory requirements. Third, it *offers recommendations* regarding necessary remedial action, areas of potential weakness to monitor closely, and targeted areas of need, among other things. Finally, it *provides a baseline* against which future performance can be measured and linked to implemented improvement processes. These objectives combine to achieve the goal of the baseline assessment: to facilitate identification of problem areas and elimination of potential areas of abusive or fraudulent conduct. This baseline information gathering is distinct from audits, which evaluate the compliance program in operation or investigate an alleged violation. *(See also Chapter 2, No. 4 – Monitoring and Auditing.)*

In most organizations the compliance officer cannot conduct such an extensive organization-wide assessment alone. The assistance and support of an executive-appointed baseline review team would be suggested. This team may be the core group that ultimately will grow into the compliance committee, especially with the intelligence gathered from the internal assessment. Among its members there should be experience and expertise in law, finance, and the organization's operations. Consideration may be given to having an outside expert conduct the assessment, but such a decision will depend on your organization's size and culture. The compliance officer must be actively involved in the baseline assessment, even with outside specialists to provide the background and an understanding of the organization's operations.

How the assessment is conducted is culture- and resource-dependent, but this is a very effective first step for any organization's compliance program efforts. The first place to start is by reviewing any previous problem areas. Those issues identified by the regulatory agencies in their various settlements, penalties and/or fines. But it is just as important to include individualized risk areas as well. Check for and review any previous assessment, investigative reports, or evaluations conducted by outside regulatory entities. In addition, a look at existing policies will help determine any potential vulnerabilities. Are the policies and procedures appropriate? Are they being followed? A review of actual practices related to those procedures as well as to regulation is also in order. It is important that the baseline assessment analyze current education and training practices. Whatever the findings, staff will need to be educated on any changes resulting from existing training efforts as well as implementation of the compliance program. If there is weakness in the education program, it must be addressed as early as possible.

Trade and professional associations for the organization's industry can also provide information on current issues and emerging trends. These can include potential risk areas for consideration in developing the baseline risk assessment.

There are two primary sources of information for the assessment team: documents and staff. One approach is to start with interviewing managers, those best acquainted with the organization's operations. This is also an excellent opportunity to personalize the compliance program. Open the discussion with information about yourself and plans for the compliance program. Be sure to explain the purpose of the interview and the assessment and, if possible, mention what follow-up processes will be used. First, ask general questions, and then move on to a more detailed level later. This is your opportunity to explore what is currently occurring and to identify the managers' areas of concern. Some sample topics for discussion are as follows:

- Functions and/or controls that are subject to frequent breakdowns
- The current compliance environment in the department
- The process for monitoring issues and how that information is reported
- How new regulations or policy changes are distributed
- How the department is trained on internal and external requirements
- How the department's policies and procedures are developed and updated
- How is it verified that policies and procedures are being accurately implemented

- General methodology for communicating with direct reports.

It is strongly advised that you take detailed notes during these interviews. These will assist the team later in evaluating the information.

As noted above, review of documentation should begin with an in-depth look at any previous audit reports or evaluations. Check carefully to see if recommendations were communicated to the appropriate parties and whether they were in fact implemented. In addition, a review of policies and procedures should be done to determine whether accurate. Check, too, for availability of policies and procedures; i.e., does staff have ready access? Do they know they have access? Finally, it is important that training records be a part of the baseline assessment in order to determine if education has been adequate and whether existing systems can handle implementation of a compliance program. Training information may need to be solicited from individual departments if there is no centralized system. Education plans, syllabi, handouts, and all attendance records should be reviewed and evaluated. Include information on outside education as well.

Once the assessment is complete, the team will prepare a report for executive management. This report will identify any noncompliance standards and practices and make recommendations regarding remedial action. It is the starting point for developing the compliance program, and it will serve as the "benchmark" to which future assessment can be compared. Observations and all recommendations should be discussed with executive management prior to preparation of any report to identify any unexplored issues or concerns. The goal is a complete, accurate, and realistic assessment that addresses the needs of the organization. How the information collected is shared with senior leadership and those who participated will need to be determined by the organization.

If at any point during the assessment process egregious errors or outright fraudulent activities are identified, it is of paramount importance to consult internal and/or outside legal counsel. The improper activities also should be stopped immediately.

6. Develop Mission and Goals

Once the compliance staff is in place, it must function as a team toward a common goal. Building that sense of camaraderie within the compliance department is critical before you can begin building a compliance camaraderie organization-wide. As always, the size and setting of the organization as well as logistical issues must be considered. The first focus should be dedicated to drafting a mission statement for the department, a mission statement that is consistent with the organization's mission statement. It is important for everyone in the compliance department to understand that fit and to be reading from the same page.

> *Sample Compliance Department Mission Statement*
>
> The Office of Compliance strives to provide the highest quality of education and monitoring to assure integrity in the ethical and legal aspects of business practice for the organization and its community.

Goals for the upcoming year (which need not be a calendar year) and a review of progress toward current year goals should also be a focus. Be sure to identify a realistic number of goals and goals that are achievable and measurable. Not all goals will be measured quantitatively, but when discussing goals, explore with staff how success will be measured. Goals need not be directly tied to specific problems.

Sample Compliance Department Annual Goals

- To develop and maintain clear lines of communication with key personnel throughout the organization
- To provide diverse educational opportunities to meet the demands of the organization and its community
- To create and maintain quality compliance resources that are easily accessible
- To promote the Code of Ethics for Compliance and Ethics Professionals
- To elevate awareness and increase participation regarding compliance issues throughout the community
- To expand the collaborative relationships with key stakeholders

- To maintain an open-door policy fostering confidentiality and trustworthiness
- To ensure compliance in all of the organization's activities.

The more active a role the staff takes in developing the mission statement, especially the goals, the more they will feel "ownership" of them and the more likely they will succeed.

However the goals are determined, it is important they be effectively and regularly communicated to the department staff. Discussing and measuring progress along the way, with updates at regular staff meetings, will contribute significantly toward progress. Assigning a department "liaison" for each goal also can contribute to ownership and stimulate progress. Should any goals come to the department from executive management, these should be communicated and incorporated into tracking and measuring practices.

Annual compliance reports help to provide detailed annual compliance status reviews to the board of directors or the governing committee and the organization's executive management. An annual report is a different document, one meant for all staff. The Compliance Annual Report is an opportunity to communicate your mission and goals to the organization. It is also an opportunity to talk about the organization's compliance success stories, thereby reinforcing positive images of compliance and fostering support. Thanking compliance champions and those who came forward to identify problems provides positive reinforcement organization-wide. The Compliance Annual Report need not be glitzy and expensive. The point is to get the word out and to build support. Use the data that you've gathered, and show your enthusiasm. It can be contagious.

7. Next Steps After Implementation

Once a compliance program is up and running, it needs ongoing evaluation and updating based on those results. Getting a handle on regular review can be difficult; indeed, it can be as daunting as getting started).

1. Look to your compliance program. Meet with the compliance committee to discuss and document current position and possible next steps.

2. Take baby steps. Make preliminary attempts at next steps with full knowledge that there may be some false steps along the way.

3. Review lessons learned. Gather the take-home lessons for those preliminary attempts.

4. With your compliance committee, decide how to incorporate what you've learned with what you still need to do. Compliance is an ongoing process.

4

Tailoring Your Compliance Program

The compliance program must be tailored to fit your organization. There is not a "one size fits all" program. As we have discussed, you need commitment from the top actively supporting your program, financial support including necessary staffing, and a continual assessment of your program. Once you understand the organization's needs, then you can fit your plan to the organization. The code of conduct should be the focal point of your program.

1. Communication

Communication of your program's expectations and goals is key to its success. The communication must be clear, concise, and creative. Much of compliance-related information can be difficult to understand because so much of it is buried in thousands of pages of regulations. The written standards of conduct and policies and procedures should be clear and easy to understand, and they should be distributed to all staff. What good is the compliance plan if no one in the organization knows it exists? Compliance may not be an exciting topic for everyone, so be creative and use many methods to communicate. Be creative, and keep your program fresh and exciting.

The 3 Cs of Communication

- Clear
- Concise
- Creative

There are many ways to communicate the compliance message. Communicating can include going to each site of operations and listening to their overall challenges in the field; conducting one-on-one training; or using role play exercises during education sessions. Look for ways your organization celebrates successes, and tap into them. If your organization has a holiday party, consider contributing in some visible and fun way—a skit or karaoke song for example, if that fits your organization's culture. Trinkets with a compliance theme or message can be popular, assuming the budget allows. Cups or pens can be inexpensive enough to allow distribution to all employees. Posters, brochures, and wallet cards can also be effective. Consider a compliance open house or a "road show" to other departments. Fax or e-mail alerts targeted to affected departments are a good way to get attention. (Just be sure to use them sparingly; if used too often they will lose their sense of urgency.) Your reporting system is also a communication tool. Make sure all employees know about the reporting systems you have in place. And as much as is possible, get back to them with results—results of investigating questions, complaints, results of compliance successes, results of audits. Remember: communicate, communicate, communicate!

The most important communication device is an open-door policy in the compliance department. Help managers to be open to employee questions. Encourage all staff to stop by the compliance office with questions or concerns. Compliance personnel, managers, and supervisors should keep their eyes and ears open constantly to pick up on the conversations that employees have and the subjects they bring up that may have revealing compliance-related information. The accessibility of the compliance officer will communicate much more than the specifics of regulations and laws; it will communicate a sense of mutual trust and common goals.

2. Continual Evaluation

You have your plan, and you have communicated it to all staff. Now what do you do with it? The compliance plan should be reviewed at least annually. There may be a new regulation or law, new guidelines from regulatory agencies. Changes will need to be made. Ask yourself if what you have in writing is really occurring. Is it working? Could it be improved? The compliance oversight committee should take an active role in this process.

In addition, all policies and procedures need to be monitored. A complete review of each policy should be done at least annually. Such a task can obviously become overwhelming, so you may want to consider a predetermined schedule for reviewing policies and procedures. Certain policies can be reviewed in January, for example, another batch in April and so on. Here, too, the compliance committee can be of help. As you look at the policies and procedures, consider if they are still necessary. It's possible a new policy has superseded an existing one. Have circumstances changed to warrant revising a policy or procedure? Are the policies and procedures effective? And as we have discussed, policies that are written and not followed can lead to trouble. Be sure to evaluate whether all employees are aware of the policies and procedures pertinent to their positions. You can't expect them to follow policies if they don't know about them.

Benchmarking against yourself is also a good way to measure and evaluate your program. Your annual report provides one regular statistical summation that can be used to develop benchmarking statistics. You might track and compare the number of educational programs delivered or number of employees trained in a given period, for example. Or compare the number of issues reported and the number of issues later substantiated. Just be sure you collect consistent data so comparisons of results are viable.

Evaluating for Success

To determine if your efforts at building a compliance program are a success, the following tactics can yield important information:

- Annual review of written compliance program
- Continual review of individual policies and procedures
- Benchmarking against your own statistics
- Comparing your program's progress to the industry's.

3. Measuring Effectiveness

How can you tell if your program is effective? What is effectiveness? It has not been defined in exact words, but generally, a program can be considered effective if it includes a basic design infrastructure that includes the seven elements covered in Chapter 2:

1. Written standards of conduct and policies and procedures
2. Designation of a chief compliance officer and other appropriate bodies
3. Effective education and training
4. Audits and evaluation techniques to monitor compliance
5. Establishment of reporting processes and procedures for complaints
6. Appropriate disciplinary mechanisms
7. Investigation and remediation of systemic problems.

Effectiveness Measures

Additional measures of effectiveness can also be used. As identified by Compliance 101 educational seminar participants, here are more ideas for measuring effectiveness:

- Comparing issues year to year
- Tracking and trending complaints
- Tracking corrective actions and no reoccurrence of related issues
- Reviewing concurrent audits
- Comparing educational session pre- and post-tests
- Tracking external agencies' findings, fines and penalties
- Reviewing organizational survey results
- Analyzing audit results
- Ensuring compliance has been integrated into organization discussions.

But how do you get there? One method requires the identification of three measures of effectiveness: structure, process, and outcome. Structure refers to the capacity of an organization to provide services, including staffing levels and policies and procedures. Process refers to performance measures or the manner in which business is conducted. And outcome addresses observable, measurable results. William Altman concludes that "the context of compliance program effectiveness should be clearly understood before reaching conclusions about the effectiveness of any given program."[6] That context is critical. Different measures may be required for annual evaluation than those required for an identified improvement.

Six Steps to Building a Framework for Effectiveness

1. Identify compliance risk areas.

2. Identify how the organization addresses the identified risk areas by categorizing compliance program elements into structure, process and outcome measures.

3. Assess the "maturity" of the compliance program before drawing definitive conclusions about effectiveness.

4. Evaluate the extent to which structure, process and outcome measures of effectiveness are viewed as "linked" by the compliance program.

5. Evaluate the extent to which the compliance program is "dynamic" and continuously changes in response to internal and external factors.

6. Measure compliance program effectiveness against both regulatory agencies' and organizational goals.

7. Identify the organization's "risk intelligence" in comparison to the baseline assessment conducted at the initial phases of the compliance program.

4. Organizational Fit

The importance and value of the code of conduct cannot be emphasized enough. The code of conduct must address your organization's culture, its beliefs, its ethical position. The code of conduct—and the compliance program—must understand, accept, and "live" the organization's mission, vision, and objectives. Your code of conduct may include photographs of staff. It may have sample questions and sample situations specific to the scope and setting of your organization. It may be distributed at an all-staff meeting with a speech from the chairman of the board. Or it might be distributed by individual managers at a regular department meeting. You must be sensitive to your organizational needs and incorporate compliance in ways that will be consistent with the existing way of doing things. Culture will drive your program. While there may be things you want to change, remember that change can be difficult for many people. To the extent you can keep it familiar, your job will be a bit easier.

5. Advancing Your Program

A compliance program is never finished; it should always be a work in progress. You must work to expand your program to fit the needs of your organization. Never be satisfied with the status quo. Look at the big picture. Add new areas to your program; many programs begin with a key risk, but other areas also need attention. As new information is released from industry and/or regulatory agencies, your program will need to expand to encompass all these changes. The compliance officer needs to constantly be on the lookout for ways to enhance and broaden the compliance program.

6. Change

If a compliance program is never finished, if it is a work in progress, then change will be the one sure constant in the compliance officer's job. There are several meanings for the word "change." One is "to make different." Among other definitions are "to undergo a modification" and "to transform." There is nothing in the definitions to indicate how difficult change can be. But for many, change can be very frustrating. Just when you think you are done, things change. We all know that feeling, but that is what compliance is all about, and also what makes compliance one of the most exciting fields today. With that change comes new challenges. You will be challenged constantly to remain abreast of new regulations, to sense the pulse of the industry, to learn innovative ways to motivate and educate staff, to find new strategies to keep executive management informed and involved. The work isn't necessarily easy—but it is important. Through change you can make a difference.

7. Compliance Program Breaking Points

Given that compliance programs must be tailored to fit an organization and that no two compliance programs are identical, it may be difficult to evaluate how effective your organization's compliance program really is. However, organizations can readily identify when their program is suffering and has barriers to effectiveness. The following are common compliance breakdowns that could indicate the need for program modification or enhancement:

- Compliance officer has inadequate technical skills (auditing, verbal, and written communication), knowledge (finance, operations, legal requirements), compliance vision, and/or resourcefulness

- Lack of financial resources

- Lack of commitment from employees, vendors, management, CEO, and/or board of directors

- Compliance officer lacks authority to enforce standards, policies and procedures

- Compliance officer lacks a direct line of communication with the CEO and board of directors

- External resources assume compliance responsibilities to avoid accountability or integration into the organization's operations

- Conflicts of interest and/or lack of independence of compliance officer

- Conflicts of interest and/or lack of independence of auditors

- Lack of, or improper dissemination of, policies and procedures

- Inaccurate, highly theoretical, non-tailored, out-of-date policies and procedures

- Poor/incorrect/inadequate training content (in general or for the specific audience)

- Unqualified trainer or trainer not seriously teaching the compliance content

- Education sessions too long, too over-filled with information, not made to be interesting (monotone trainer, lack of multimedia use), not required, and/or not frequent enough

- Lack of variation in education (training sessions, memos, postings, one-on-one instruction, web-based training, et cetera)

- Training too heavily based on one method; e.g., web-based

- Lack of understanding of what should be reported or of the obligation to report suspected inappropriate actions

- Lack of culture of openness and non-retaliation regardless of anonymity

- Lack of ability to report issues in an anonymous way

- Fear of retaliation or retaliation itself

- Lack of follow-through with information communicated or lack of feedback regarding resolution

- Disciplinary action not consistent

- Disciplinary action plan not enforced when necessary and as stated

- Disciplinary action plan not progressive or fitting for the "crime"

- Auditing and monitoring schedule not sufficient (substance/number/frequency), not followed, or not dynamic/changing to fit new situations, fraud alerts, industry developments

- Auditors not trained well (in auditing techniques or content of audit), not cooperative, or not cooperated with

- Investigations not thorough/comprehensive/timely
- Immediate remediation of problem not taken
- Long-term corrective action plans not put into place
- Lack of continued monitoring into areas of proven noncompliance
- Lack of enforcement of disciplinary guidelines.

Epilogue

As you know, better than most, compliance professionals must deal with complex and cumbersome laws and regulations on a daily basis. But industry laws and regulations are not new. Today, more so than in the past, we are approaching compliance in a formal, systematic way. Armed with a mandate from regulatory agencies, our board and senior leadership, we are creating and implementing compliance programs—programs that embody and fulfill our organizations' commitment to compliance as part of providing the best possible services.

Organizational commitment is key to an effective compliance program. Commitment not only from management but from every staff member is needed to achieve a truly effective compliance program. An environment of trust is the ultimate benefit of total organizational commitment, and that trust, in turn, is what inspires cooperation and participation from all employees. In addition, appropriate and ample educational opportunities ensure that staff members have the tools to do their jobs and fulfill their responsibilities. The result is the confidence of knowing that, if there are questions or if errors are discovered, employees will come forward within the organization.

No matter what the culture of your organization, you, as a compliance professional, whether a compliance officer or a member of the compliance oversight committee, are charged with building or enhancing that atmosphere of trust. You must work toward that goal every day. Commitment begins with you.

Early on we emphasized strongly that it is better to have no policy than one that is ignored. Embodied in that message is the need for constant attention. Compliance can be a demanding task master. You aren't facing it alone, however. Remember that you have, through SCCE, among many other educational resources, literally thousands of colleagues with whom you can network. Use every resource available to find new ways for replenishing your own commitment and for enhancing your organization's commitment.

We hope this book has provided some help and guidance for you as you launch your career in compliance and begin your compliance program. We are here to help—no matter what new challenges the future brings.

Debbie Troklus
Sheryl Vacca
Society of Corporate Compliance and Ethics

Appendices

Appendix A.1

Sample Letter to Vendors

Dear Vendor Colleague:

Our organization is committed to building and supporting an organization that demonstrates honesty, integrity, ethics, and best practices. In an effort to strengthen this commitment, we have established a corporate compliance program and developed a Standards of Conduct. These Standards of Conduct are our attempt to offer guidance for the complex legal and business issues we face every day and to provide the overall principles for our system. The standards outlined apply to all employees. We also expect them to apply to all our vendor, supplier, and affiliate colleagues.

Please direct your attention to the conflicts of interest section of the standards. You can see this standard clearly prohibits employees and their families from receiving gifts or any other consideration of value from a person or organization that does business or may want to do business with our organization or its affiliates. The only exception is a gift of nominal value extended as a business courtesy, such as sales promotion items or occasional business-related meals or entertainment of modest value. In an effort to help our employees abide by this standard, we are requesting that all vendors, suppliers, and affiliates refrain from offering our employees any items other than ones of nominal value.

Thank you. If you have questions or would like to discuss the Standards for Business Conduct handbook or the Conflict of Interest standard, please do not hesitate to contact me.

Sincerely,
[Name]
Compliance Officer

Appendix A.2

Sample Non-Retaliation/Non-Retribution Policy

Background/Purpose

- XXX has implemented a compliance program that promotes the highest standard of ethical and legal conduct. Standards of conduct and procedures for faculty members, residents, and staff are implemented to guide this effort.

- XXX believes that positive employee relations and morale can be achieved best and maintained in a working environment that promotes ongoing open communication between supervisors and their employees. Open and candid discussions of employee problems and concerns are encouraged.

- XXX believes employees should express their problems, concerns, and opinions on any issue and feel that their views are important. To that end, a policy that will encourage employees to communicate problems, concerns, and opinions without fear of retaliation or retribution will be implemented.

Policy

1. All employees are responsible for promptly reporting actual or potential wrongdoing, including an actual or potential violation of law, regulation, policy, or procedure.
2. The office of compliance will maintain an "open door policy" to allow individuals to report problems and concerns.
3. The office of compliance will act upon the concern promptly and in the appropriate manner.
4. The compliance hotline (1-xxx-xxx-xxxx) is designed to permit individuals to call, anonymously or in confidence, to report problems and concerns or to seek clarification of compliance-related issues.

5. Employees who report concerns in good faith will not be subjected to retaliation, retribution, or harassment.

6. No employee is permitted to engage in retaliation, retribution, or any form of harassment against another employee for reporting compliance-related concerns. Any retribution, retaliation, or harassment will be met with disciplinary action.

7. Employees cannot exempt themselves from the consequences of wrongdoing by self-reporting, although self-reporting may be taken into account in determining the appropriate course of action.

Procedures

1. Knowledge of actual or potential wrongdoing, misconduct, or violations of the compliance plan must be reported immediately to management, the compliance office, or the compliance hotline.

2. All managers must maintain an open-door policy and take aggressive measures to assure their staff that the system truly encourages the reporting of problems and that there will be no retaliation, retribution, or harassment for doing so.

3. Departmental administrators must provide a copy of this policy to all employees.

4. A copy of the policy must be posted in every department/division.

5. If employees have concerns, they should be addressed in the following order:
    1. Immediate supervisor
    2. Department manager
    3. Department head/director

6. If an employee feels uncomfortable with the above, the employee should report concerns directly to the compliance office or the hotline.

7. All concerns will be investigated within 30 days.

8. Confidentiality regarding employee concerns and problems will be maintained at all times insofar as legal and practical, informing only those personnel who have a need to know.

Appendix A.3

Sample Search Warrant Response Policy
(might not apply in some countries)

Statement

XXX recognizes that the government has increased its scrutiny of organizations by deliberately focusing on practices it considers fraudulent and abusive. It has a number of techniques at its disposal to use when investigating suspected fraudulent activity. Those techniques include grand jury subpoenas, civil investigative demands, civil subpoenas, and search warrants. Among these techniques, the use of search warrants has grown in popularity among government investigators for a variety of reasons, thus increasing the likelihood that the organization, its Office of Compliance, or other officers may be served with a search warrant. People have the right to be secure against unreasonable searches and seizures. A search may be conducted only upon a finding of probable cause. Probable cause to conduct a search is based on a review of all of the circumstances surrounding a situation and whether a reasonable person has an honest belief that the objects sought are linked to the commission of a crime and that those objects will be found in the place to be searched and the items to be seized. The investigating official has no discretion to determine what should be seized or searched; the official must follow the description on the face of the search warrant.

Policy

It is the policy of the organization to cooperate with the government's execution of a search warrant within the bounds of the law. The organization recognizes that access to an investigating officer possessing a valid search warrant cannot be refused; however, the organization further recognizes that it is not legally required to relinquish all rights of ownership or provide access to objects and areas not defined in the search warrant. The organization, therefore, sets forth the following guidelines for responding to a search warrant and encourages all departmental entities to adopt this or a similar policy.

Procedure

Should the Office of Compliance or a XXX department governed by the compliance plan receive a search warrant, the following steps shall be taken:[7]

1. The Director of the Office of Compliance (hereafter "director") shall request to see the search warrant, and the affidavit of probable cause, if available. The director shall carefully review, and copy, the search warrant and affidavit to identify the areas of the search.

2. The investigating official(s) will be confined to the areas where the records specified in the search warrant are located. The investigating official(s) will be given access to only those records, items, and areas specified in the warrant.

3. Following the arrival of the investigating official(s), the director or his or her designee shall immediately notify the division head, or his or her designee, and the general counsel.

4. The director or his or her designee shall discharge all nonessential personnel for the day. Personnel shall be instructed that absent a subpoena directed at each individual, they are under no obligation to answer any questions asked by the investigating official(s).

5. The director or his or her designee shall remain with the investigating official(s) at all times. Except to answer questions pertaining to the location of documents, or other questions wholly unrelated to the search (for example, location of copy machines, coffee machines, lavatories, et cetera), the director or designee shall not answer any questions asked by the investigating official(s) unless the general counsel is present.

6. Should the investigating official(s) attempt to enter unauthorized areas or search or review documents not specified in the warrant, the director or his or her designee shall strongly and clearly object to the investigating official(s)' request. If the investigating official(s) ignore the objections of the director, the director shall continue to object throughout the investigating official(s)' review of the objected-to material. The compliance officer or his or her

designee should carefully document the items which he or she objected to and the nature and extent of all objections.

7. The director and/or his or her designee shall closely monitor the activity of the investigating official(s):

   a. The investigating official(s) should not remain alone but should be chaperoned at all times by the director or his or her designee;

   b. The investigating official(s)' activities should be closely observed and notes made by the director and/or his or her designee of the items and areas searched and the items seized;

   c. The director and/or his or her designee should create a contemporaneous detailed inventory of all items or documents seized;

   d. The director and/or his or her designee shall observe the investigating official(s)' search only but shall not in any way impede, assist, explain, or otherwise answer questions posed by the investigating official(s).

8. The director and/or his or her designee shall advise the agents about what material is required in order to allow the Office of Compliance to carry out its business following the departure of the investigating official(s). The director and/or his or her designee shall obtain the investigating official(s)' permission to:

   e. Make copies of all documents essential to the continued conduct of business of the Office of Compliance or XXXX department prior to turning over the material to the investigating official(s);

   f. Copy files prior to turning them over to the investigating official(s) if those computer files are requested as a part of the search;

   g. Duplicate any other material essential to the continued conduct of the business.

9. The director and/or his or her designee shall request from the investigating official(s) a copy of their inventory that they have created pursuant to the search and seizure. The director and/or his or her designee shall ask that to the extent possible, if the inventory identifies the boxes and contents of boxes by numbers and documents therein, that the copy of said inventory be turned over the director.

10. Following the investigating official's departure from the premises, the director and/or his or her designee shall review the inventory of items seized with the division head and general counsel. General counsel, the division head, and the director shall formulate a plan for debriefing any employees and other organization officials as soon as conveniently possible.

Appendix A.4

Sample Compliance Officer Job Description

COMPLIANCE OFFICER JOB DESCRIPTION

The Position

The compliance officer provides direction and oversight of the compliance program. The compliance officer is responsible for identifying and assessing areas of compliance risk; communicating the importance of the compliance program to the executive management and the board of directors; preparing and distributing the written code of conduct setting forth the ethical principles and policies which are the basis of the compliance program; developing and implementing education programs addressing compliance and the code of conduct; implementing a retaliation-free internal reporting process, including an anonymous telephone reporting system; and collaborating with executive management to effectively incorporate the compliance program within system operations and programs and to carry out the responsibilities of the position.

Primary job duties and responsibilities

- Creating and implementing an effective compliance program

- Ensuring that the compliance program effectively prevents and/or detects violation of law, regulations, organization policies, or the code of conduct

- Regularly reviewing the compliance program and recommending appropriate revisions and modifications, including advising administrative leadership and the board of directors of potential compliance risk areas

- Coordinating resources to ensure the ongoing effectiveness of the compliance program

- Implementing and operating retaliation-free reporting channels, including an anonymous telephone reporting system available to all employees, volunteers, customers, and vendors

- Developing educational programs for all employees, agents, contractors, or others working with the organization

- Ensuring that the internal controls are capable of preventing and detecting significant instances or patterns of illegal, unethical, or improper conduct by employees, agents, contractors, or others working with the organization

- Ensuring that the system has effective mechanisms to reasonably determine that persons either promoted to or hired in management and certain other sensitive and/or responsible positions (to be designated) do not have a propensity to violate laws and regulations or engage in improper or unethical conduct in their designated areas of responsibility

- Providing input and/or direction to human resources policies and procedures and the performance appraisal and incentive programs to ensure that improper conduct is discouraged and that support of any conformity with the compliance program is part of any performance evaluation process for all employees

- Coordinating as appropriate with outside legal counsel, conducting or authorizing and overseeing investigations of matters that merit investigation under the compliance program

- Overseeing follow-up and, as applicable, resolution to investigations and other issues generated by the compliance program, including development of corrective action plans, as needed

- Tracking all issues referred to the compliance office

- Developing productive working relationships with all levels of management

- Presenting periodic and annual reports on the compliance program to the board of directors

- Developing and implementing, upon an approval by executive management and the board of directors, an annual review of an update to the compliance plan

- Reporting on a regular basis to the compliance committee on matters involving the compliance program. Additionally, the compliance officer at his or her discretion is expected to regularly report issues to the CEO and board of directors

- Working with administrative leadership to provide adequate information to staff to ensure that they have the requisite information and knowledge of regulatory issues and requirements to carry out their responsibilities in a lawful and ethical manner

- Ensuring that all contracts contain language which is corporate compliant

- Representing the compliance committee, including developing appropriate agendas, reports, and information as directed from time to time by the committee

- Performing other duties as assigned by the CEO Principal Duties

- Oversee, coordinate, and monitor the day-to-day compliance activities of the organization

- In collaboration with internal stake holders, establish a company compliance manual; maintain and supplement the manual as necessary

- Establish, supervise, and train teams of department compliance officers responsible for identifying compliance issues at the departmental level; ensure appropriate communication for compliance issues between local and system levels, if applicable

- Develop and coordinate appropriate compliance training and education programs for all employees; ensure and understand the company's commitment to comply with all laws, regulations, company policies, and ethical requirements applicable to the conduct of the business; assess the need for additional training and education and develop appropriate compliance programs

- Develop, coordinate, and/or oversee internal and external audit procedures for the purpose of monitoring and detecting any misconduct or noncompliance; if any misconduct or noncompliance is detected, recommend a solution and follow up to ensure that the noncompliance is resolved

- Formalize and monitor a system to enable employees to report any noncompliance without fear of retribution, ensuring that the reporting system is adequately publicized and that allegations of noncompliance are investigated and responded to promptly. This mechanism, if developed, will be in compliance with country-specific laws regarding reporting mechanisms

- In consultation with the human resources department, help ensure that there is a mechanism in place for disciplining instances of noncompliance (including the failure to prevent, detect, or report any noncompliance), appropriate to the nature and extent of the deviation and ensure consistency in the application of disciplinary action

- Work with the human resources department to ensure a work force with high ethical standards, including the establishment of minimum standards for conducting appropriate background and reference checks on potential employees

- In conjunction with the legal department, interface and, when appropriate, negotiate with external regulatory agencies

- Report to the compliance committee at its regular meetings, or as otherwise when necessary, on any significant compliance issues to ensure appropriate discussion of such compliance issues and to ensure that appropriate action is taken

- Carry out all duties and responsibilities as assigned by the compliance committee.

Job Specifications: Education and Experience Required

- CCEP preferred with experience in industry-specific content and specific knowledge of fraud and abuse issues

- Auditing/CPA experience a plus

- Experience in dealing with compliance issues preferred

- Strong verbal and written communication skills

- Strong influencing skills and perseverance in investigating.

Appendix A.5

Sample Audit Review Form

To be completed for a compliance program audit, either routine or random.

Upon completion, please return to: _____

Date of review: _____

Review conducted by: _____

Process or procedure to be reviewed: _____

_____

_____

Reason:

☐ New Regulation ☐ Routine Review ☐ Fraud Alert ☐ Random Review

☐ Other: _____

Site location / department(s): _____

Scope of review *(include sample size, attach additional sheets if necessary)*: _____

_____

_____

Results of review *(include any attachments)*: _____

_____

_____

_____

Specific issues or risks identified: _____

_____

_____

Has a work plan been initiated? ☐ Yes *(if yes, attach copy)* ☐ No

Resolution of issue: _____

_____

_____

Signature/Title/Date: _____

Appendix A.6

Sample Confidentiality Statement

I understand and agree that, in connection with the performance of my duties as a member of the compliance oversight committee, I will be engaged in activities of a confidential nature, including but not limited to, participating in reviews and evaluations of internal examinations, evaluations, and self-evaluations of the policies, practices, and procedures of this organization. I further understand that, in this capacity, I will be expected to receive and/or to become privy to information of a confidential nature, including but not limited to, financial statements, trade-secrets, strategic plans, contracts with private parties, and other documents and statistics which go to the issue of compliance with policies, procedures, statutes and regulations, and other information of a confidential nature. I further understand that I will be called upon to evaluate such information, in part, by the application of laws, regulations, and policies, as well as policies of this organization, to the information which I receive. I understand that my position as a member of this committee is one which demands the highest trust and that the organization's policies and procedures, as well as, in some instances, specific statutes, regulations, and governmental policies, protect the confidentiality of certain records and information which I will be reviewing by prohibiting their disclosure in any manner. In addition to any duty of confidentiality or non-disclosure imposed on me by specific statutes, regulations, and governmental policies, I agree to keep secret, and not to disclose to others nor make any personal use of whatsoever, either during my service on said committee or at any time thereafter, of any said confidential information and to hold any such documents and/or information, regardless of nature, in strictest confidence. I understand that any violation of this confidentiality statement will subject me to disciplinary action, up to and including removal from this committee and/or termination of employment. I further understand that my duty to maintain the information in confidence imposed hereunder shall survive my resignation or termination from this committee or my termination of employment for whatever reason from this organization.

_____
Signature / Date

_____
Printed Name / Title

_____
Witness Signature / Date

Appendix A.7

Sample Complaint Information Sheet
Questions and Concerns Call Log Sheet

Name: _____

Person/Dept Calling: _____

Date/Time: _____

*Call #:_____

Question or Concern: _____

_____

_____

Action Taken: _____

_____

_____

_____

Follow-Up Date: _____

_____

_____

Follow-Up Action:_____

_____

_____

_____

*How to make call # assignment: The month plus initials of the person taking the call plus the # of call. Log knowledge-based concerns or questions, *i.e.*, billing, policies, education, financial statements, contracts, et cetera (for example: 08 DT 001).

Appendix A.8

Sample Compliance Issue Follow-Up Form

(Optional: Can be used with the "Sample Complaint Information Sheet—Questions and Concerns Call Log Sheet")

Date: _____

Name of individual if not anonymous: _____

Contact information: _____

Call #: _____

Department, if known: _____

Issue Discussed: _____

_____

_____

_____

Action Taken: _____

_____

_____

_____

_____

Findings / Resolution: _____

_____

_____

_____

_____

Report Made By: _____

Date: _____

Appendix A.9

Audit Review Plan Templates

Example 1

20xx Audit Review Plan

Area	Scope	Projected Timing	Assigned Accountability for Audit
Fraud Risk Management*	Evaluation of the potential for the occurrence of fraud and how the organization manages fraud risk	1st Quarter	Internal Audit and Finance
Conflict of Interest/ Conflict of Commitment	Assessment of the adequacy and clarity of existing policies and procedures designed to identify and manage potential financial conflicts of interest and conflicts of commitment by both employees	2nd Quarter	Compliance and Legal
Compensated Outside Professional Activities	Assessment of compliance with policies and procedures on reporting compensated outside professional activities	3rd Quarter	Compliance
Ethics and Compliance Programs*†	Evaluation of the design and infrastructure of the organization's ethics and compliance program	3rd Quarter	Third Party (compliance can't be independent)
Executive Compensation	Review of Executive Compensation	3rd Quarter	Internal Audit, Compliance
Safety of Mobile Oil Platforms†	Review for compliance to policy on environmental safety on mobile oil platforms	3rd Quarter	EH & S with third party (for independence)
Data Privacy	Review for compliance to policy on mobile devices	4th Quarter	Compliance and Privacy Officer

* Audit required by XX regulatory, accreditation or other agency
† Audit will be outsourced due to subject matter needed or need for independence

Example 2

Chart below depicts compliance audit coverage across the organization. It demonstrates breadth of coverage while indicating where major business functions or business processes might collectively command a larger amount of our effort.

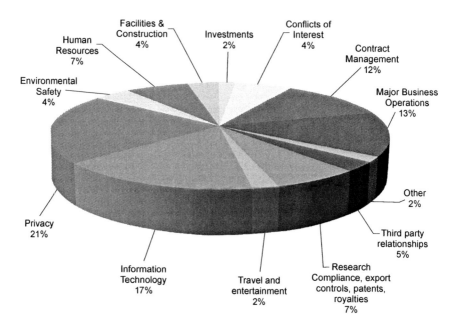

Distribution of Planned Projects

Example 3

Lists all the planned compliance audit and monitoring projects at each location - the progress and status of these projects are reported quarterly.

List of Compliance Audit and Monitoring Projects

Business Unit (6 FTE) – Audits	Estimated Hours	Estimated Completion Quarter	Accountability (department to conduct activity)
Work for Others / Sponsored Projects	350	Q3	Compliance
FY12 Cost Allowability	650	Q1	Compliance
Third Party Relationships	400	Q2	Legal and Compliance
Export Controls	350	Q4	Legal and Compliance
IT Security	400	Q2	IT and Third Party
Distributor Contract Compliance	350	Q4	etc.
Construction Safety	400	Q3	etc.
Contract Compliance with External Agency Projects	500	Q2	
Data Protection - Privacy	300	Q1	
Conflict of Interest Process	250	Q1	
Executive Compensation	300	Q2	
Compliance to new Regulatory Requirement	300	Q3	

Business Unit – Monitoring	Estimated Hours	Estimated Completion Quarter
Business Process Review - Division TBD	750	TBD
Business Process Review - Division TBD	750	TBD
Total Planned Hours – LBNL	**6,050**	

Appendix A.10

Sample Board of Directors Resolution

Office of the Secretary and Chief of Staff

To Members of the Committee on Compliance and Audit:

ACTION ITEM

For Meeting on: _____

RECOMMENDATION

Regent _____ recommends that the Committee on Compliance and Audit recommend to the Regents that, following a presentation in the Committee regarding the proposed Ethics and Compliance program by Senior Vice President _____, the Regents approve the following resolution:

WHEREAS, the Regents of _____ made the decision in May 2006 to establish a university-wide program of corporate compliance and established the new position of Senior Vice President – Chief Compliance and Audit Officer, an officer of the corporation, by amending the Bylaws and Standing Orders accordingly; and

WHEREAS, President _____ strongly endorses and recommends that _____ have a robust ethics and compliance program, and

WHEREAS, Senior Vice President – Chief Compliance and Audit Officer _____ assumed the position in October 2007 and has developed the proposed program and structure for an effective Ethics and Compliance Program for _____; and

WHEREAS, voluntary adoption of such a program is considered a best business practice that will serve to enhance the public trust and meet expectations of the Regents and external stakeholders by demonstrating the Regents' commitment to good stewardship of federal, state and private resources; and

WHEREAS, the proposed program, in consultation with the campuses, includes a reasonable timeline for development of all requisite elements of an effective Ethics and Compliance program including:

1. Written standards of conduct as well as appropriate policies and procedures;

2. Oversight by the Regents' Committee on Compliance and Audit and the Senior Vice President – Compliance and Audit with the primary responsibility for the campus ethics and compliance activities assumed by the Chancellors and delegated to the Campus Compliance Officer, as appropriate. Advice on compliance matters and risk mitigation activities will be provided from the campus risk committee and the Ethics and Compliance Risk Council;

3. Development and implementation of regular, effective education and training programs, as well as mandated education such as sexual harassment prevention, conflicts of interest, ethics and compliance, and other areas of concern,

4. Effective communications and processes maintained for reports of potential and/or perceived compliance matters or improper governmental activities with timely responses which provide the ability for a complainant to remain anonymous and free from retaliation;

5. Development and maintenance of compliance systems and controls that can be objectively assessed, monitored, and audited for effectiveness;

6. Assurance that management is enforcing appropriate disciplinary action for those who have violated university policies, procedures, or applicable legal requirements; and

7. Assurance that management is taking appropriate corrective action and remedial measures when problems are identified to resolve and prevent reoccurrence of those problems; and

WHEREAS, Senior Vice President – Chief Compliance and Audit Officer _____ and the Office of Ethics, Compliance and Audit Services are primarily responsible to assure that campus responsibilities are executed related to ethics and compliance matters and to assess and monitor that campus compliance systems and controls are effective, and

WHEREAS, the proposed program committee infrastructure includes a broad cross-section of individuals from all university locations and specific risk areas; and

WHEREAS, performance metrics will be developed to assess and evaluate identification of risks and the performance of related compliance systems to ensure rules, regulations, _____ policies and other compliance requirements are met,

NOW, THEREFORE, BE IT RESOLVED, that the Regents of _____ do approve and adopt the Ethics and Compliance Program and structure shown in Attachment I.

BACKGROUND

The Regents created the role of Senior Vice President – Compliance and Audit (SVP) as a corporate officer reporting directly to the Regents through the Committee on Compliance and Audit in _____ with the intent that a comprehensive Ethics and Compliance structure would be developed under the leadership of this role In _____, the Regents appointed _____ to the SVP position. Upon arrival, SVP _____ consulted with _____ leadership to identify four major risk areas for initial focus and created a project team to conduct a compliance activities inventory for the four areas at all campus locations. Insight and information gained from this process provided a foundation for understanding the complexity and scope of the university as well as the many regulatory requirements that govern its operations.

The Department of Health and Human Services ("HHS") and other federal funding agencies have outlined program guidance on the structure of an effective ethics and compliance program based on the Federal Sentencing Guidelines, listing the seven elements contained in the proposed program and identified in the language of the resolution. Since _____ is a recipient of significant federal, state and private research dollars, it was determined that federal guidance would be used as the foundation for establishment of the _____ Ethics and Compliance Program.

The proposed program and structure recognizes the size and complexities of _____ and takes into account the need for a university-wide approach sufficient to address these complexities. Respect for the individual and unique culture of each _____ location, while providing a venue for communication and leveraging good works within the _____ system, are important aspects of the program structure. If the Regents approve the program and structure at this meeting, next steps will include implementing the approved model at all locations, identifying further performance metrics for the university at all locations, further developing each element of the program and continuing communication with the Regents related to progress of the implementation, reporting on performance metrics and on high risk areas. The proposed Ethics and Compliance Program is described in further detail in the attached document, "_____ Ethics and Compliance Program Plan" ("Plan").

The Federal Sentencing Guidelines require that a governing board be "knowledgeable about the content and operation of the compliance and ethics program." For that reason, the proposed program and its structure is to be presented at a meeting of the Committee on Compliance and Audit to which all Regents are invited. Following the presentation, it is recommended that the Committee on Compliance and Audit recommend to the Regents that it approve and adopt the proposed program by approving the resolution.

Appendix B

Code of Ethics for Compliance and Ethics Professionals

PREAMBLE

Compliance and ethics programs serve a critical role in helping to prevent and detect misconduct at and by organizations and to promote ethical business environments. The development and rigorous implementation of effective compliance and ethics programs protects investors, consumers, the business community and the public at large. Compliance and ethics professionals (CEPs) understand that the services we provide require the highest standards of professionalism, integrity and competence. The following Code of Ethics expresses the profession's recognition of its responsibilities to the general public, to employers and clients, and to the profession. The Code of Ethics has been adopted by the membership of the Society of Corporate Compliance and Ethics to provide guidance and rules to all CEPs in the performance of their professional responsibilities.

The Code of Ethics consists of two kinds of standards: Principles and Rules of Conduct. The Principles are broad standards that provide a framework for the more detailed Rules of Conduct. The Rules of Conduct are specific standards that prescribe the minimum level of professional conduct expected of CEPs. Compliance with the Code is expected both of the individual professional and of the professional community. It depends primarily on the CEP's own understanding and voluntary actions, and secondarily on reinforcement by peers and the general public.

Commentary is provided for some Rules of Conduct, which is intended to clarify or elaborate on the meaning and application of the Rule. The following conventions are used throughout the Code:

- "Employing organization" includes the employing organization and clients;

- "Law" or "laws" includes all national, state, provincial and local laws and regulations, court orders and consent agreements;

- "Misconduct" includes both illegal acts and unethical conduct; and

- "Highest governing body" of the employing organization refers to the highest policy and decision-making authority in an organization, such as the board of directors or trustees of an organization.

Principle I

Obligations to the Public

Compliance and ethics professionals (CEPs) should abide by and promote compliance with the spirit and the letter of the law governing their employing organization's conduct and exemplify the highest ethical standards in their professional conduct in order to contribute to the public good.

R1.1 CEPs shall not aid, abet or participate in misconduct.

R1.2 CEPs shall take such steps as are necessary to prevent misconduct by their employing organizations.

Commentary: The CEP's actions to prevent misconduct must, of course, be legal and ethical. Where a CEP has done what he or she can to prevent misconduct within the bounds of the law and business ethics, but is nonetheless unsuccessful in preventing misconduct, he or she should refer to Rule 1.4.

R1.3 CEPs shall exercise sound judgment in responding to or cooperating with all official and legitimate government investigations of or inquiries concerning their employing organization.

Commentary: While the role of the CEP in a government investigation may vary, the CEP shall never obstruct or lie in an investigation.

R1.4 If, in the course of their work, CEPs become aware of any decision by their employing organization which, if implemented, would constitute misconduct, the professional shall: (a) refuse to consent to the decision; (b) escalate the matter, including to the highest governing body, as appropriate; (c) if serious issues remain unresolved after exercising "a" and "b", consider resignation; and (d) report the decision to public officials when required by law.

Commentary: The duty of a compliance and ethics professional goes beyond a duty to the employing organization, inasmuch as his/her duty to the public and to the profession includes prevention of organizational misconduct. The CEP should exhaust all internal means available to deter his/her employing organization, its employees and agents from engaging in misconduct. The CEP should escalate matters to the highest governing body as appropriate, including whenever: a) directed to do so by that body, e.g., by a board resolution; b) escalation to management has proved ineffective; or c) the CEP believes escalation to management would be futile. CEPs should consider resignation only as a last resort, since CEPs may be the only remaining barrier to misconduct. A letter of resignation should set forth to senior management and the highest governing body of the employing organization in full detail and with complete candor all of the conditions that necessitate his/her action. In complex organizations, the highest governing body may be the highest governing body of a parent corporation.

Principle II

Obligations to the Employing Organization

Compliance and ethics professionals (CEPs) should serve their employing organizations with the highest sense of integrity, exercise unprejudiced and unbiased judgment on their behalf, and promote effective compliance and ethics programs.

R2.1 CEPs shall serve their employing organizations in a timely, competent and professional manner.

Commentary: CEPs are not expected to be experts in every field of knowledge that may contribute to an effective compliance and ethics program. CEPs venturing into areas that require additional expertise shall obtain that expertise by additional education, training or through working with others with such expertise. CEPs shall have current and general knowledge of all relevant fields of knowledge that reasonably might be expected of a compliance and ethics professional, and shall take steps to ensure that they remain current by pursuing opportunities for continuing education and professional development.

R2.2 CEPs shall ensure to the best of their abilities that employing organizations comply with all relevant laws.

Commentary: While CEPs should exercise a leadership role in compliance assurance, all employees have the responsibility to ensure compliance.

R2.3 CEPs shall investigate with appropriate due diligence all issues, information, reports and/or conduct that relates to actual or suspected misconduct, whether past, current or prospective.

Commentary: In organizations where other professionals (such as the Legal Department) are responsible for investigation of suspected misconduct, CEPs satisfy this Rule by reporting suspected misconduct to such professionals in accordance with established reporting procedures.

R2.4 CEPs shall keep senior management and the highest governing body informed of the status of the compliance and ethics program, both as to the implementation of the program and about areas of compliance risk.

Commentary: The CEP's ethical duty under this rule complements the duty of senior management and the highest governing body to assure themselves "that information and reporting systems exist in the organization that are reasonably designed to provide to senior management and to the board itself timely, accurate information sufficient to allow management and the board, each within its scope, to reach informed judgments concerning both the corporation's compliance with law and its business performance." In re Caremark International Inc., Derivative Litigation, 1996 WL 549894, at 8 (Del. Ch. Sept. 25, 1996).

R2.5 CEPs shall not aid or abet retaliation against any employee who reports actual, potential or suspected misconduct, and shall strive to implement procedures that ensure the protection from retaliation of any employee who reports actual, potential or suspected misconduct.

Commentary: CEPs should preserve to the best of their ability, consistent with other duties imposed on them by this Code of Ethics, the anonymity of reporting employees, if such employees request anonymity. Further, they shall conduct the investigation of any actual, potential or suspected misconduct with utmost discretion, being careful to protect the reputations and identities of those being investigated.

R2.6 CEPs shall carefully guard against disclosure of confidential information obtained in the course of their professional activities, recognizing that under certain circumstances confidentiality must yield to other values or concerns, e.g., to stop an act which creates appreciable risk to health and safety, or to reveal a confidence when necessary to comply with a subpoena or other legal process.

Commentary: It is not necessary to reveal confidential information to comply with a subpoena or legal process if the communications are protected by a legally recognized privilege (e.g., attorney client privilege).

R2.7 CEPs shall take care to avoid any actual, potential or perceived conflicts between the interests of the employing organization and either the CEP's own interests or the interests of individuals or organizations outside the employing organization with whom the CEP has a relationship. CEPs must disclose and ethically handle conflicts of interest and must remove significant conflicts whenever possible. Conflicts of interest may create divided loyalties. CEPs shall not permit loyalty to individuals in the employing organization with whom they have developed a professional or a personal relationship to interfere with or supersede the duty of loyalty to the employing organization and/or the superior responsibility of upholding the law, ethical business conduct and this Code of Ethics.

Commentary: If CEPs have any business association, direct or indirect financial interest, or other interest that could influence their judgment in connection with their performance as a professional, the CEPs shall fully disclose to their employing organizations the nature of the business association, financial interest, or other interest. If a report, investigation or inquiry into misconduct relates directly or indirectly to activity in which the CEP was involved in any manner, the CEP must disclose in writing the precise nature of that involvement to the senior management of the employing organization before responding to a report or beginning an investigation or inquiry into such matter, and must recuse him or herself from such investigation or inquiry, if appropriate. Despite this requirement, such involvement in a matter subject to a report, investigation or inquiry will not necessarily prejudice the CEP's ability to fulfill his/her responsibilities in that regard.

R2.8 CEPs shall not mislead employing organizations about the results that can be achieved through the use of their services.

Commentary: CEPs should not create unreasonable expectations with respect to the impact or results of their services.

Principle III

Obligations to the Profession

Compliance and ethics professionals (CEPs) should strive, through their actions, to uphold the integrity and dignity of the profession, to advance the effectiveness of compliance and ethics programs and to promote professionalism in compliance and ethics.

R3.1 CEPs shall pursue their professional activities, including investigations of misconduct, with honesty, fairness and diligence.

Commentary: CEPs shall not agree to unreasonable limits that would interfere with their professional ethical and legal responsibilities. Reasonable limits include those that are imposed by the employing organization's resources. If management of the employing organization requests an investigation but limits access to relevant information, CEPs shall decline the assignment and provide an explanation to the highest governing authority of the employing organization. CEPs should diligently strive to promote the most effective means to achieve compliance.

R3.2 Consistent with Rule 2.6, CEPs shall not disclose without consent or compulsory legal process confidential information about the business affairs or technical processes of any present or former employing organization. Such disclosure could erode trust in the profession or impair the ability of compliance and ethics professionals to obtain such information from others in the future.

Commentary: CEPs need free access to information to function effectively and need the ability to communicate openly with any employee or agent of an employing organization. Open communication depends upon trust. Misuse and abuse of the work product of compliance and ethics professionals poses a serious threat to compliance and ethics programs. CEPs shall not use confidential information in any way that violates the law or their legal duties, including duties to their employing organizations. When adversaries in litigation use an organization's own self-policing work against it, the credibility of CEPs may be undermined. CEPs are encouraged to work with legal counsel to protect confidentiality and to minimize litigation risks. It is not necessary to reveal confidential information to comply with compulsory legal process if the confidential information is protected by a legally recognized privilege (e.g., attorney-client privilege).

R3.3 CEPs shall not make misleading, deceptive or false statements or claims about their professional qualifications, experience or performance.

R3.4 CEPs shall not attempt to falsely damage the professional reputation of other compliance and ethics professionals.

Commentary: In order to promote collegiality and civility in the profession, CEPs shall not make any statements concerning other CEPs that are defamatory in nature.

R3.5 CEPs shall maintain their competence with respect to developments within the profession, including knowledge of and familiarity with current theories, industry practices, and laws.

Commentary: CEPs shall pursue a reasonable and appropriate course of continuing education, including but not limited to review of relevant professional and industry journals and publications, communication with professional colleagues and participation in open professional dialogues and exchanges through attendance at conferences and membership in professional associations.

Code of Ethics Development Committee

Joseph E. Murphy, CCEP (Committee Co-Chair)
Of Counsel, CSLG
Co-Founder and Senior Advisor, Integrity Interactive
Co-Editor, *ethikos*

Rebecca Walker (Committee Co-Chair)
Partner, Kaplan & Walker LLP

Urton Anderson
Associate Dean for Undergraduate Programs and
Clark W. Thompson Jr. Professor in Accounting Education,
McCombs School of Business, The University of Texas at Austin

Michael Horowitz
Litigation partner, member of the Business Fraud and Complex Litigation Group, Cadwalader, Wickersham & Taft LLP
Commissioner, U.S. Sentencing Commission

Shelley Milano

Marjorie Doyle
Practice Leader, Ethics & Compliance Solutions, LRN

Special thanks to the Health Care Compliance Association's Code of Ethics Development Committee

Jan Heller, PhD

Mark Meaney, PhD

Joseph E. Murphy, Esquire

Jeffrey Oak, PhD

Glossary of Compliance Terms

APEC — Asian-Pacific Economic Cooperation is an intergovernmental group formed to facilitate economic growth, cooperation, trade and investment in the Asia-Pacific region. It operates on the basis of non-binding commitments, open dialogue and equal respect for the views of all participants.

Attestation — The affirmation by signature, usually on a printed form, that the action outlined has been accomplished by the individual signing; e.g., the individual has read the code of conduct and agreed to adhere to its principles.

Attorney-Client Privilege (US mainly, but may apply to some other countries) — A legally accepted policy that communication between a client and attorney is confidential in the course of the professional relationship and that such communication cannot be disclosed without the consent of the client. Its purpose is to encourage full and frank communication between attorneys and their clients.

Chain of Command — The hierarchy of reporting structure within an organization, which assumes all issues will be presented first to one's immediate supervisor.

Chief Audit Executive (CAE) — A high level independent corporate executive with overall responsibility for internal audits.

Commonwealth of Independent States (CIS) — A regional organization whose participating countries are former Soviet Republics, formed to coordinate powers in the realm of trade, finance, law, and security.

Chief Ethics and Compliance Officer (CECO) — See Chief Compliance Officer.

Chief Compliance Officer (CCO) — In larger, more complex organizations, there may be multiple compliance officers. The highest ranking compliance officer, typically at the organization's headquarters, may be designated the chief compliance officer. Also known as the Chief Ethics and Compliance Officer (CECO).

Compliance Officer (CO) — The senior manager responsible for managing the compliance and ethics program. Also known as the Compliance and Ethics Officer (CEO), or sometimes the Ethics Officer (the focus of this role includes compliance).

Compliance Program (CP) — A system of management steps to prevent and detect misconduct. Also known as the Compliance and Ethics Program.

Computer Based Training (CBT) — A method of training that relies on computer software to allow each employee to self-pace through the curriculum.

Consent Decree — See Corporate Integrity Agreement.

Corporate Integrity Agreement (CIA) — A negotiated settlement between an organization and a governing authority in which the provider accepts no liability but must agree to implement a strict plan of supervised corrective action. Also known as a Consent Decree.

Due Diligence — A legal term that represents the amount of effort required to meet legal standards. Meeting due diligence standards requires an amount of effort based on the risk involved.

Ethics Program — Companies sometimes refer to "ethics programs" instead of compliance programs. Ethics programs are generally values oriented, and focus on doing the right or moral thing, not just what is legal.

European Union (EU) — An economic and political union of member states that are located primarily in Europe.

Generally Accepted Accounting Principles (GAAP) — The common set of accounting principles, standards and procedures that companies use to compile their financial statements. Many nations follow the International Financial Reporting Standards, which are set by the International Accounting Standards Board.

Hotline; Helpline — A common reporting system, administered in house or by outside consultants, giving anonymous telephone access to employees seeking to report possible instances of wrongdoing. May not be allowed or certain restrictions may apply in some countries.

Human Resources (HR) — The business function that oversees selection, training, assessment and transactional tasks (e.g., payroll, benefits) of an organization's workforce.

Independent Private Sector Inspector General (IPSIG) — An independent, private sector firm employed by an organization (voluntarily or by compulsory process) to ensure compliance with relevant law and regulations, and to uncover and report unethical and illegal conduct within the organization.

International Accounting Standards Board (IASB) — The independent, accounting standard-setting body of the International Financial Reporting Standards Foundation. The IASB is responsible for developing the International Financial Reporting Standards, which aims to establish a common global standard for methods of financial reporting. More than 113 countries currently require or permit IFRS reporting.

Institute of Internal Auditors (IIA) — An international professional association that offers training, certification and other services for internal auditors.

International Organization for Standardization (ISO) — A network of national standards bodies that develops and promotes voluntary international standards for major sectors of industry and commerce.

Law Council of Australia — This association represents the legal profession at the national level, to speak on behalf of its constituent bodies on national issues, and to promote the administration of justice, access to justice and general improvement of the law.

Mergers and Acquisitions (M&A) — The term used to indicate when organizations either merge on equal terms — go forward as a single new company — or when one company acquires another and clearly establishes itself as the new owner.

Organisation for Economic Cooperation and Development (OECD) — This international organization collects and analyzes data on a broad range of topics and works with governments to develop economic and social policy that foster prosperity and fight poverty.

Retaliation or Retribution — Retaliation or retribution refers to efforts to punish someone for raising ethical or compliance questions or reporting misconduct. Handling of these issues may vary by country.

Society of Corporate Compliance and Ethics (SCCE) — The professional association dedicated to helping compliance professionals through education, networking opportunities, and other information resources. Its mission is "to champion ethical practice and compliance standards in all organizations and to provide the necessary resources for compliance professionals and others who share these principles."

Self-reporting — A term used to indicate when, having identified actual wrongdoing, an organization informs the applicable regulatory authority. May not apply in some countries, or there may be another method for this activity to occur.

Transparency International (TI) — This independent organization works with partners in government, business and the private sector to put measures in place that fight corruption.

Endnotes

1. Working Group on Bribery in International Business Transactions, "Annex II: Good Practice Guidance on Internal Controls, Ethics, and Compliance," in *Recommendation of the Council for Further Combating Bribery of Foreign Public Officials in International Business Transactions*; Paris: Organisation for Economic Cooperation and Development, 2010.

2. Organisation for Economic Cooperation and Development, "OECD Convention on Combating Bribery of Foreign Public Officials in International Business Transactions: Ratification Status as of 20 November 2012," (http://www.oecd.org/daf/anti-bribery/antibriberyconventionratification.pdf).

3. Donna C. Boehme and Joseph E. Murphy, "International Recognition for Compliance and Ethics Programs: The 2010 OECD Good Practice Guidance on Internal Controls, Ethics and Compliance," in *The Complete Compliance and Ethics Manual*, Minneapolis: Society of Corporate Compliance and Ethics, p. 6.26.

4. Society of Corporate Compliance and Ethics and Health Care Compliance Association, *The Evolving Role of the Chief Compliance and Ethics Officer*, Minneapolis: Society of Corporate Compliance and Ethics and Health Care Compliance Association, October 2010.

5. C. Ideker, "How much should you spend on Compliance Programs?", *Today's Corporate Compliance*, 1:3, pp. 6-7.

6. W. Altman, "Six Steps to Building a Framework for Effectiveness," *Journal of Health Care Compliance*, 2:3.

7. See Steven M. Kowal, "Execution of a Criminal Search Warrant by the FDA - Effective Preparation and Response," *Food and Drug Law Journal* 52:117 (1997).

About the Authors

Debbie Troklus, CHC-F, CCEP-F, CHRC, CHPC, is Managing Director for Aegis Compliance and Ethics Center, where she advises clients on a wide variety of compliance related topics including compliance program implementation, compliance program effectiveness reviews, coding and billing, audit, education development and delivery, investigations, IRO services and interim and/or outsourced compliance work. She currently serves on the board of the Health Care Compliance Association and was President in 2000. She also serves on the advisory board of the Society of Corporate Compliance and Ethics and is the current president for the Compliance Certification Board.

Sheryl Vacca, CCEP-F, CCEP-I, CHC-F, CHPC, CHRC, is Senior Vice President and Chief Compliance and Audit Officer for the University of California. In this role, Sheryl directs and oversees the University's system-wide compliance and internal audit programs applicable to all UC communities including ten campuses, five medical centers, the Berkeley National Laboratory, (Lawrence Livermore National Lab and Los Alamos National Lab LLP (indirect)), ANR and the Office of the President. Sheryl is a board member of the Health Care Compliance Association, and advisory board member of the Society of Corporate Compliance and Ethics. Sheryl has presented or written on compliance and/or internal audit topics internationally.